DISTANCE EDUCATION SYMPOSIUM 3:

LEARNERS AND LEARNING

Selected Papers Presented at
The Third Distance Education Research Symposium

The Pennsylvania State University
May 1995

Edited by

Chère Campbell Gibson

Number 13 in the series   **Research Monographs**

American Center for the Study of Distance Education
The Pennsylvania State University
110 Rackley Building
University Park, PA 16802

The American Center for the Study of Distance Education is a collaborative effort of the College of Education and the Division of Continuing and Distance Education.

These papers were presented at the Third Distance Education Research Symposium, which was funded in part by AT&T.

**The American Center for the
Study of Distance Education**
The Pennsylvania State University
110 Rackley Building
University Park, PA 16802

ISBN 1-877780-16-2

Table of Contents

Preface

Maintaining the Momentum

I am delighted to welcome readers to ACSDE Research Monograph No. 13, and trust that as you read the following articles, written by the leading North American researchers and thinkers about distance education, you will find much to inspire and inform you.

This monograph, Learners and Learning, is one of a series of four, the others being Instruction, Policy and Administration, and Course Design. Each monograph contains a set of articles that have been developed and edited over the past year, based on papers prepared in May 1995 for the ACSDE's Third Distance Education Research Symposium. Each monograph has been shaped and nurtured by an editor, or pair of editors, and I extend thanks to Chère Campbell Gibson, Associate Professor in the Department of Continuing and Vocational Education at the University of Wisconsin-Madison, for editing Learners and Learning.

I have given this preface the title "Maintaining the Momentum." This is because I think it is important for us to remember the precedents for this particular work, to have a sense of where it is leading us, and to appreciate that what is written here is part of an on-going, indeed, historical process.

This process began in 1986 with the founding of *The American Journal of Distance Education (AJDE)*, and the establishment soon after of the American Center for the Study of Distance Education. The basic idea of the Center and purpose of *The Journal* has been to bring people together. In the United States the study of distance education, like its practice, has been highly fragmented, with little sense of community, for example, among persons researching correspondence education, education by broadcasting, and by teleconferencing. At the American Center we have tried to provide a number of vehicles for researchers, practitioners, and students who are willing to look beyond technology, who wish to identify and research the learning, instructional design, evaluation, managerial, and policy questions in distance education.

One of the first of these vehicles was the July 1988, "First American Symposium on Research in Distance Education." This was a meeting of around forty people, most of whom had shown their interest in distance education research by having an article published in *AJDE*. They were all known to the editor of *AJDE*, but not to one another. From that meeting emerged a network of persons having a better understanding of where their piece of the distance education research agenda fitted with what was going on in the rest of the field, as well as having a common sense of what needed to be done. This was the agenda for distance education research, broken down into the themes of administration and organization, learning and learner support, course design and instruction, and theory and policy.

Thirty two papers of the First American Symposium on Research in Distance Education were published in *Contemporary Issues in American Distance Education* (Moore 1990).

Following the success of the First Symposium, ACSDE used the same format in November 1990 to organize a similar event but this time focusing on the need to articulate an agenda for distance education research that was international. The first International Symposium on Distance Education Research was held in Macuto, Venezuela, prior to the 15th World Conference of The International Council for Distance Education. Again there were around fifty participants, but this time they came from a dozen countries. Once again the focus was on the state of the research and the agenda for the years ahead, though this time the question was how colleagues could collaborate internationally, not just nationally. Papers from this Symposium were published in ACSDE Research Monograph No. 5.

The impetus towards international collaboration at the Macuto symposium had one very important consequence for the evolution of distance education as a field of study and research. This was the setting up of an electronic network, known as Distance Education Online Symposium (DEOS), one of the first in distance education. By 1996, DEOS has grown to be a network of more than 4000 participants in some sixty countries.

A Second American Symposium on Research in Distance Education was held in May 1991, bringing together in equal numbers participants from the 1988 meeting with others who had published research in *AJDE* or DEOS during the intervening years. Sixteen states were represented as well as Canada. Participants addressed the themes: What have been the results of research since the First Symposium? What are the questions for further research? A poll of participants resulted in the following "top issues":

- Interaction of learner attributes and instructional methods
- Strategies for introducing innovations in course design/delivery
- Need for and effectiveness of interaction (faculty-student, student-student)
- Faculty/administrator development (Moore et al. 1991)

The papers of this Second Symposium were published as ACSDE Research Monograph Nos. 4, 8, and 9, which are available from ACSDE.

From reading these few notes, I hope it will be apparent why I said that the 1995 Symposium should be seen in its historical context. Context will show us the progress we have made, and point to the directions ahead. Just ten years ago there was no defined field of distance education research, and it has taken just ten years to reach the level of sophistication recorded in the pages of this monograph. Context also helps us understand why we are not better than we are. Our growth has been fast, and uncontrolled, and it is not surprising that some seeds, planted hurriedly and hastily brought to blossom, have not flourished. Context, provided by the papers that record the discussions at previous symposia, should help us recognize the sturdy themes, those that have been reiterated as one set of discussants has given way to another. Since each paper cites the sources of its author's thinking, we would be foolish to pass over the opportunity of identifying the pedigree underlying any question that may now appear to be of interest. These are documents that cry out to be used as a means of providing theoretical underpinning for any new venture.

So now, I invite you to turn to Chère Gibson's introduction, and then the papers provided in this, the papers from ACSDE's Third American Symposium on Research in Distance Education. I expect there will be a Fourth Symposium before very long, and that perhaps you will wish to attend. Perhaps you will be able to refer to the themes identified in previous Symposia, and show how your research has advanced that agenda. If so, I will be very happy to see you.

Michael G. Moore

References

Moore M., ed. 1990. *Contemporary Issues in American Distance Education*. Oxford: Pergamon Press.

Moore, M., M. Thompson, P. Dirr, eds. 1991. Report on The Second American Symposium on Research in Distance Education. University Park, PA: The American Center for the Study of Distance Education.

1 Introduction

Chère Campbell Gibson

Introduction

Learners and learning are truly the raison d'etre for distance education. One might question this statement however, based on a reading of the research literature in North America. An analysis of the first eight volumes of *The American Journal of Distance Education* with its 117 total research articles finds only seventeen (14.5%) devoted to learners and learning. Of the eighty-two research articles published in the same period of time in the *Journal of Distance Education* from Canada, sixteen (19.5%) focus on learners and learning (Coldeway 1995). Research, for the most part, has focuses on those variables which might be termed process variables, for example, instructional systems design models, instructional technologies, academic support, formal feedback, and the like (Calvert 1986). Learners and learning are tangential. What is evident is the need for a definition of learning at a distance and a systematic program of research which focuses on learners and learning at a distance, rather than isolated efforts. Further this research program should bridge theory and practice towards the end of enhancing the quality of distance teaching and learning.

The papers which follow exemplify the range of research on learners and learning. In the first four articles, we see an emphasis on those unique characteristics of the learner and their relationships to learning processes employed and outcomes achieved. Chris Olgren's research highlights the relationships among and between learner motivations, cognitive processes and resultant learning outcomes. Roger Bruning's focuses on self-efficacy and its impact on learning choices and achievement outcomes. The loneliness of the distance learner is the subject of Rudy Pugliese's exploration while Susan May's research provides insight into the distance learner's active process of creating and applying knowledge and of meaning making. Research by Yolanda Gayol and Catherine Fulford with coauthor Shuqiang Zhang highlight the interactive processes in learning while Michaeleen Davis and Kathryn Atman explore conation and goal orientation in distance learning.

The monograph provides the reader with some key research findings with important implications for practice. But what research is needed to enhance the quality of distance education? Three key questions emerge: What is quality distance learning? What are quality learning outcomes? How are these quality learning processes and outcomes achieved? Based on the assumption that we can agree on a definition of distance education, it seems important to define quality distance learning—the process of learning at a distance. While we may have the beginnings of agreement in terms of what quality outcomes of distance education are, for example, satisfied learners, learners who have developed critical thinking and problem solving skills, developed an enhanced repertoire of cognitive and metacognitive strategies, learners who can understand, analyze, synthesize, and evaluate key concepts and their applications, can we agree on the processes so central to these outcomes?

Research needs to focus on, for example, the selection and implementation of learning strategies employed in distance learning contexts, the process of meaning-making for learners, an understanding of the intricacies of collaborative learning at a distance, the impact of context, including technology, on the learning processes employed, and the formation and operation of learning 'communities' across time and space.

This is not to say that research into the characteristics of more or less successful distance learners should be abandoned, in fact many would suggest that, in addition to the more static demographic variables, the more affective variables, including a number highlighted in the research in this monograph, should be explored in future research. Nor should research into the variety of intervention strategies or treatments be discontinued. Rather we should continue to explore the interaction of learner aptitudes, intervention strategies and learning contexts on both learning processes and outcomes to better understand how quality distance learning might be enhanced.

Quality distance learning and quality distance education research are inextricably intertwined. In order to meet our ultimate goal of enhancing learning at a distance, we need to develop a comprehensive program of research which focuses on distance learning and a solid cadre of researchers trained to conduct quality research in the future. Lastly, we need to continue to develop a strong bridge between research and practice.

Chère Campbell Gibson

References

Calvert, J. 1986. Research in Canadian distance education. In *Distance Education in Canada,* eds. I. Mugridge and D. Kaufman, 94–110. London: Croom Helm.

Coldeway, D. 1995. A research agenda for distance education: Setting targets for learning and learners. Paper presented at the Third Research Symposium in Distance Education, May, University Park, Pennsylvania.

2 Cognitive Strategies in Independent Learning

Christine H. Olgren

Background

Each year thousands of adults enroll in independent study courses in higher education to learn at a distance. The courses provide a structure for learning, typically in the form of print materials, study guides, and assessment activities. However, more research is needed on how adults learn from text, the cognitive skills needed to carry out the learning process, and the relationship between cognition and outcomes. As Morrison (1989) observed, removing barriers to effective learning and improving the quality of outcomes begins with the question "What and how are people learning and what affects that process?"

Several studies in distance education have examined cognitive learning processes (Marland, Patching, and Putt 1992; Bernt and Bugbee 1993; Valcke et al. 1993) and students' approaches to learning (Morgan, Taylor, and Gibbs 1982; Harper and Kember 1986; Strang 1987; Ekins 1992). While that research has provided a better understanding of the learning process, there are many unanswered questions about the cognitive dimensions of distance learning. Some distance educators have discussed the potential usefulness of cognitive psychology research and theory, including the concepts of constructivism (Garrison 1993; Candy 1991; LeBaron and Bragg 1994), situated learning (Hummel 1993), and cognitive strategies for text comprehension (Howard 1985). However, few studies have applied cognitive learning theory, which is based in classroom contexts, to distance education settings.

Conceptual Framework

This study's conceptual framework drew from learning strategy research in cognitive psychology, which focuses on how people mentally process information and construct knowledge in memory. Learning strategies are defined as thoughts and behaviors that are intended to influence how a person learns, thinks, and motivates self in order to carry out a learning task (Weinstein and Mayer 1986). Studies indicate that capable learners use various cognitive strategies to select, organize, and integrate information as well as metacognitive strategies to plan and regulate learning. Ultimately, capable learners are said to be self-directed in having the capacity to design and carry out their own learning activities (Thomas and Rohwer 1986; Derry and Murphy 1986; Glaser 1990). Studies also link cognitive strategies to the quality of learning, where differences in depth of processing result in qualitatively different outcomes in understanding, retention, and integration with prior knowledge (Dansereau 1985; Pintrich and Johnson 1990; McDaniel and Kearney 1984).

Most learning strategy theory in cognitive psychology is based on a constructivist perspective, which contends that meaning and knowledge are constructed by the learner through a process of relating new information to prior knowledge and experience. Learning is viewed as an active, purposeful, and meaning-generating process that occurs within the learner (Shuell 1986). In other words, learning involves the transformation of information into meaningful knowledge, where cognitive strategies serve to activate mental processes and prior knowledge to generate meaning from learning events (Jonassen 1985).

Cognitive strategy research appears to hold promise for understanding the cognitive dimensions of distance learning. However, few studies have examined adult learning in a natural setting, and there appear to be no studies of distance learners. Most prior research has been experimental or quasi-experimental, conducted in classroom settings, with participants being either children or traditional college students age eighteen to twenty-five. The findings, therefore, may not be generalizable to other contexts.

Methodology

Because it was uncertain if previous research would apply to adult learners in a natural, non-classroom setting, an interpretive case study methodology was used to explore the learning process from the learners' perspective. Qualitative data were gathered in interviews with twenty adults enrolled in an independent study course in marketing, as part of an extended degree program to earn a baccalaureate in business administration. The course was self-paced and a required part of the core curriculum. It included a textbook and study guide divided into six modules. Each module of coursework comprised a reading assignment, a written learning exercise, and a multiple choice examination.

Because learners enrolled at different times and progressed at different paces, sequential criterion-based sampling (Goetz and LeCompte 1984) was used to interview students who were twenty-five years or older and at least mid-way through the coursework. Interviewed were fifteen women and five men, ages twenty-five to fifty-one, with an average age of thirty-seven. All were Caucasian, resided in urban and rural communities throughout Wisconsin, and all but one were employed full-time. Prior to enrolling in the program, most had completed at least two years of college, although half had not been in school for ten years or more. The course and sample were judged by program administrators to be typical of the extended degree program.

The interview was semi-structured, conversational in style, and averaged seventy-five minutes. Participants were asked to describe how they went about reading and studying one module of course material—what they did and why. They were also asked about their motivations and perceptions. As a stimulated recall technique, participant's learning materials were used as a physical point of reference during the interview to help reconstruct the learning experience and to provide secondary observational data (Ericcson and Simon 1980). The interviews were audiotaped and transcribed. Data analysis included techniques of pattern coding, inter-coder reliability, matrix analysis, audit trail, and peer examination of findings (Miles and Huberman 1984; Merriam 1988).

Findings

This paper summarizes major research findings. A full account of the study, including interview segments, is found in Olgren (1992).

Types of Cognitive Strategies. The findings revealed that learners engaged in various cognitive activities in reading and studying course material, and those activities generally paralleled the types of cognitive strategies identified in prior research (Weinstein and Mayer 1986). As shown in Table 1, learners used four types of cognitive strategies that served different primary functions.

Selection strategies were directed to focusing attention and to identifying relevant information. Learners employed two kinds of selection strategies: 1) focusing externally on cues in the textbook and study guide to identify what the author or instructor thought important to learn; or 2) focusing internally on the learner's own needs and interests to identify information important to the learner. Not surprisingly, students said the primary reason for focusing on external cues was to identify material to learn for the exam. Assessment demands, therefore, had a major effect on how and what people learned.

Table 1. Types of Cognitive Strategies

Selection Strategies
Function: To focus attention and to identify relevant information
Examples: Focusing externally on text cue or study guide aids, focusing internally on personal needs and interests

Rehearsal Strategies
Function: To remember information by repetition
Examples: Memorizing, repeating, highlighting, copying, reading aloud, reviewing

Organization Strategies
Function: To build connections within the text
Examples: Determining main ideas and relationships, outlining, listing, classifying, ordering, diagramming, comparing, contrasting, getting an overview, structured notetaking

Elaboration Strategies
Function: To expand the meaning and to build connections to prior knowledge/experience
Examples: Paraphrasing, summarizing, visualizing, associating ideas with examples, generative notetaking, creating analogies or metaphors, relating to prior learning, applying to work or everyday life, roleplaying, brainstorming, reflecting, inferencing, evaluating usefulness, discussing, questioning, explaining, problem-solving

Learners also employed many kinds of rehearsal, organization, and elaboration strategies directed to remembering and understanding the text. Learners used rehearsal strategies to reproduce and remember factual information. Their organization strategies were directed mainly to analyzing text structure and interpreting the logical meaning of the material, although learners differed in the degree they penetrated the underlying structure—theme, main ideas, principles, relationships, and supporting details. Learners' elaboration strategies were directed to going beyond the text to construct new meanings and to build connections to prior knowledge or experience. Elaboration strategies varied widely, ranging from simple associations, to typical study strategies of paraphrasing and summarizing, to higher-level strategies involving inferencing, analogical reasoning, reflective thinking, and applications to work or daily life.

Patterns of Cognitive Strategies and Purposes. The findings revealed that cognitive strategies could not be divorced from the learner's purpose in using them. The essence of a strategy was that it consisted of an action—a thought or behavior—that was carried out to accomplish a goal or purpose. Each specific strategy, such as outlining, role-playing, or creating analogies, was carried out with a particular goal in mind in doing one part of a learning task. In addition, specific strategies worked together as a set—or coherent pattern—to accomplish a general purpose for reading.

Three variations in reading patterns were found, with each pattern showing a different strategy emphasis and purpose in reading. The three patterns were conceptualized as different approaches to learning and called: 1) a reproducing approach; 2) a comprehension approach; and 3) an application approach. Participants were almost evenly divided among the three groups. As summarized in Table 2, strategy patterns for the three groups differed in where mental effort was focused—in rehearsing, in organizing, or in elaborating the text. The learners' strategy emphasis also showed variations in depth of processing, ranging from passive and shallow processing at a level of verbatim reproduction to active and elaborative processing at a level of knowledge construction and integration. Comparing the three groups, the deepest learning involved a combination of higher-level organization and elaboration strategies directed to understanding and applying the material.

Table 2. Differences in Strategies and Outcomes

	Reproducing approach	Comprehension approach	Application approach
Strategy emphasis	Rehearsal	Organization	Organization and elaboration
Cognitive purpose	To remember	To comprehend	To understand and apply
Knowledge gained	Retained little	Retained basic theme or main idea	Retained general understanding of how ideas worked or were applied
Knowledge used	Little or none	Little or none	Three or more ideas or skills that were used in work or daily life
Perceive	Little or none	Little or none	Some or high in learning new skills, attitudes, or perspectives

Learning Outcomes. To discover what students learned from their own viewpoint, the study asked learners about their perceptions of outcomes. As summarized in Table 2, different approaches to learning led to qualitatively different outcomes in knowledge gained, knowledge used, and value, as perceived by the learner. The outcomes were also consistent with the depth of processing expressed by the learners' cognitive strategies and purposes. Learners who were most active in elaborating and organizing the content (an application approach) achieved a significantly higher quality outcome than others.

Factors Influencing Strategy Choices. The study found several factors that influenced learners' strategy choices. The factors included goal orientation, perceptions of task value, perceptions of exam requirements, perceptions of learning, and strategy knowledge. As summarized in Table 3, differences in these factors helped to explain why learners differed in strategy emphasis and cognitive purposes.

Table 3. Factors Affecting Strategy Choices

	Reproducing approach	Comprehension approach	Application approach
Goal orientation	Entirely extrinsic	Mostly extrinsic	Equally extrinsic and intrinsic
Perceived task value	Low	Low or some	Some or high
Perceptions of exam	Required exact and detailed facts	Required comprehension of concepts and fundamentals	Required conceptual understanding and application of principles
Perceptions of having learned	When you recall the information later or do well on an exam	When it makes sense and you can apply it	When you can apply it or your way of seeing or doing things changes
Strategy knowledge	Unaware of alternatives; low-level strategies; typical way of learning	Aware of alternatives; adapted strategies to task demands and preceptions	Aware of alternatives; preferred high level strategies to achieve valued goals

- Goal Orientation: A learner's goal orientation involved aims, interests, and motives in relation to the module, course, and extended degree program. A goal orientation, then, showed the learner's intentions not only for the immediate task of learning one module of course material but also for the broader learning context in which the task was embedded. The learners in this study had goal orientations similar to those identified by Taylor, Morgan, and Gibbs (1981) in a study of British Open University students. Moreover, this study found that each approach to learning served a different goal orientation. Although students had multiple goals that were vocational, academic, and personal in nature, the goals showed a consistency in orientation towards extrinsic or intrinsic concerns. Extrinsic goals were concerned with learning as a means to some other end, such as getting a good grade, completing academic requirements, and earning a degree for job promotion. Intrinsic goals were concerned with learning the material itself for skill development, intellectual interests, challenge, or personal growth. Of the three groups of learners, those using an application approach were the most intrinsically motivated.

- Perceptions: Differences among the three groups of learners were also found in their perceptions of task value, exam requirements, and having learned (see Table 3). Using the concept of task value (Pintrich 1988), this study asked students if they found anything interesting, valuable, or useful about the module. Perceptions ranged from little or none for learners using a reproducing approach to a great deal for those using an application approach. Task value was also tied closely to attitudes toward the learning experience (independent study, academic coursework, and the extended degree program), with perceptions of low value accompanied by negative attitudes, and perceptions of high value accompanied by positive attitudes. Learners in the application group also expressed an openness to finding value or to changing their attitudes that was not characteristic of the other two groups. In addition, the interview data indicated that learners with different approaches had different perceptions of what they were expected to know for the exam. Their interpretations of the level of knowledge required for the exam differed in a way that was consistent with their approach to learning. The three groups also showed consistent differences in their perceptions of having learned, in response to a question asking how they knew when they had learned something.

- Strategy Knowledge: Strategy knowledge was conceptualized in this study as having three dimensions: awareness of alternative strategies, knowledge of strategy effectiveness in accomplishing goals, and awareness that strategy adjustments may be needed to match the learning task (Pressley, Borkowski, and Schneider 1987). The three groups of learners differed in knowledge about cognitive strategies (see Table 3), and their strategy knowledge drew on past academic experiences. Learners with a reproducing approach had the least strategy knowledge. They employed strategies in a largely habitual way that was typical of how they learned in academic situations. They routinely used rehearsal strategies, showed little awareness of alternatives, did not make strategy adjustments, and were apt to attribute problems in learning to the task itself (such as trick exam questions) rather than to their strategies. Learners with a comprehension approach were the most apt to adjust their strategies to task perceptions, although some learners were more aware of alternative strategies and made greater adjustments than others. They adjusted their strategies to the type of exam (multiple choice vs. essay), time available for study, familiarity of the content, and the content's perceived value. Learners with an application approach were aware of how they learned and had experimented with alternative strategies in the past. Although they were capable of strategy adjustments and considered alternatives, they preferred to use higher-level strategies that enabled them to achieve valued goals in learning for understanding and application.

Discussion

In investigating the experience of independent study from the learners' perspective, this research provided a window into the learning process and how adults learned from text. The learners' own descriptions told how they read and studied, their goals and aims, and their perceptions of the experience. Those descriptions, when analyzed from a cognitive strategy perspective, revealed a complex but consistent pattern of relationships among a learner's strategies, goals, perceptions, and outcomes. Cognitive strategies for reading and studying showed that the learning process involved both effort and purpose. Cognitive effort was exhibited in the ways learners used strategies for selecting, organizing, integrating, and remembering information. Learning was also purposeful. Cognitive strategies were directed to accomplishing goals, and they were affected by general aims, motives, and attitudes toward the experience. Strategies were also affected by strategy knowledge and how the learner perceived and interpreted the task. Cognitive strategies, then, were embedded in a context that involved the learner's intentions, motivations, and perceptions as well as past experiences with academic studying. Finally, different learning strategies resulted in different outcomes in terms of what was learned. A learner's cognitive strategies not only showed how learning was carried out but also revealed how differences in the learning process affected the quality of the outcome—the level of understanding, knowledge gained, and knowledge used.

Adults' natural ways of learning in this study were generally consistent with prior research on the types of cognitive strategies employed by learners in classroom settings (Weinstein and Mayer 1986). Studies have typically found that rehearsal strategies involve shallow processing at a surface level of verbatim learning, while organization and elaboration involve processing at deeper levels of meaning and understanding (Dansereau 1985; McDaniel and Kearney 1984; Bradshaw and Anderson 1982; Pintrich and Johnson 1990). The influence of motivation and perceptions on strategy choices also paralleled findings on the effects of goal orientation and conceptions of learning on surface and deep approaches (Marton and Saljo 1984). A learning strategy perspective drawn from cognitive psychology suggests a promising avenue for further research on the cognitive dimensions of distance learning. This study identified only some of the factors involved in the complex act of learning. More studies are needed to investigate distance learning with other settings, course designs, and media.

Implications for Distance Education Research and Practice

- The quality of learning: A consistent finding of this study and prior research is that the quality of learning varies widely among students. From a learning strategy perspective, quality is conceptualized as the level of understanding, integration, and application attained by the student. In this study only a third of the learners attained quality outcomes, those using an application approach. A quality of learning perspective raises questions about the aims and indicators of success in distance education practice. Using common success indicators of grades, course completion rates, and persistence rates (Paul 1990), the learners in this study would be "successful." They completed the course, earned good or passing grades, and were persisting in the degree program. However, the students' depth of learning and perceptions of outcomes suggest that other quality indicators are needed. Paul (1990) suggests two added indicators that he considers critical to the future of distance education in a knowledge society: skill development and post-course performance Although more difficult to measure, the two relate to the quality of learning—how and what students learn—or the extent to which students develop independent learning skills and gain knowledge useful for subsequent education, employment, or personal development. As this study found, students may lack cognitive skills or may learn little that is useful to them. Additional studies are needed that define quality from a learning perspective, including the students' perceptions of how and what they learn.

- Fostering mental and emotional engagement: The group of application learners in this study indicates that the deepest learning involves active mental and emotional engagement where the learner carries on a "reflective conversation" with the text, much as envisioned by Holmberg (1986). Such engagement is demonstrated by learners who use a variety of organization and elaboration strategies, including applying material to everyday life, and who are intrinsically motivated and perceive the task to have value or usefulness. How might distance educators foster active engagement in learning by students of varying abilities and motivations? This study's findings suggest that important insights into fostering learner engagement may be gained by research on how students respond to application activities involving real-world settings, simulations, or anchored instruction (Duffy and Jonassen 1991; Hummel 1993; The Cognitive and Technology Group at Vanderbilt 1993), as well as authentic forms of assessment that employ such methods as portfolios and formative diagnostics (McLellan 1993). Such practices may also improve the quality of learning by implementing Paul's (1990) aims for skill development and post-course performance.

- Developing learning capacities: The contextual nature of learning and the complex interactions among cognition, motivation, and perception suggest that the development of students' learning capacities requires more than simple advice or training on study skills. Study skills training that does not consider purpose or context may result in little skill improvement (Morgan, Taylor, and Gibbs 1982), low transfer to other contexts (Dansereau 1985), or an increase in surface learning if study skills are aimed at traditional assessment demands (Ramsden, Beswick, and Bowden 1987). Further research on the factors involved in learning would assist practitioners in designing effective interventions or support programs. Research should also examine how students respond to embedded support devices (Valcke et al. 1993), whole person approaches to learner development (Rhys 1988), and cognitive apprenticeship models (Brown, Collins, and Duguid 1989).

References

Bernt, F. M., and A. C. Bugbee, Jr. 1993. Study practices and attitudes related to academic success in a distance learning programme. *Distance Education* 14(1):97–112.

Bradshaw, G. L., and J. R. Anderson. 1982. Elaborative encoding as an explanation of levels of processing. *Journal of Verbal Learning and Behavior* 21:156–174.

Brown, J. S., A. Collins, and P. Duguid. 1989. Situated cognition and the culture of learning. *Educational Researcher* 18(1):32–42.

Candy, P. 1991. *Self-Direction for Lifelong Learning*. San Francisco, CA: Jossey-Bass.

Dansereau, D. F. 1985. Learning strategy research. In *Thinking and Learning Skills*, vol. I, eds. J. W. Segal and S. F. Chipman. Hillsdale, NJ: Lawrence Erlbaum.

Derry, S. J., and D. A. Murphy. 1986. Designing systems that train learning ability. *Review of Educational Research* 56(1):1–39.

Duffy, T. M., and D. H. Jonassen. 1991. Constructivism: New implications for instructional technology? *Educational Technology* 31(5):7–12.

Ekins, J. M. 1992. The development of study processes in distance learning students. Paper presented at the Asian Association of Open Universities September, Korea, .

Ericcson, K. A., and H. A. Simon. 1980. Verbal reports as data. *Psychological Review* 87:215–251.

Garrison, D. R. 1993. A cognitive constructivist view of distance education: An analysis of teaching-learning assumptions. *Distance Education* 14(2):199–211.

Glaser, R. 1990. The reemergence of learning theory within instructional research. *American Psychologist* 45(1):29–39.

Goetz, E. T., and M. C. LeCompte. 1984. *Ethnography and Qualitative Design in Educational Research*. Orlando, FL: Academic Press.

Harper, G., and D. Kember. 1986. Approaches to study of distance education students. *British Journal of Educational Technology* 17(3):212–222.

Holmberg, B. 1986. *Growth and Structure in Distance Education.* London: Croom Helm.

Howard, D. C. 1985. Reading and study skills and the distance learner. *Distance Education* 6(2):169–187.

Hummel, H. G. K. 1993. Distance education and situated learning: Paradox or partnership? *Educational Technology* 33(12):11–22.

Jonassen, D. H. 1985. Learning strategies: A new educational technology. *Programmed Learning and Educational Technology* 22(1):26–34.

LeBaron, J. F., and C. A. Bragg. 1994. Practicing what we preach: Creating distance education models to prepare teachers for the twenty-first century. *The American Journal of Distance Education* 8(1):5–19.

Marland, P., W. Patching, and I. Putt. 1992. Thinking while studying: A process tracing study of distance learners. *Distance Education* 13(2):193–221.

Marton, F., and R. Saljo. 1984. Approaches to learning. In *The Experience of Learning,* eds. F. Marton, D. Hounsell, and N. Entwistle. Edinburgh: Scottish Academic Press.

McDaniel, M. A., and E. M. Kearney. 1984. Optimal learning strategies and their spontaneous use: The importance of task appropriate processing. *Memory & Cognition* 12(4):361–373.

McLellan, H. 1993. Evaluation in a situated learning environment. *Educational Technology* 33(3):39–45.

Merriam, S. B. 1988. *Case Study Research in Education: A Qualitative Approach.* San Francisco, CA: Jossey-Bass.

Miles, M. B., and A. M. Huberman. 1984. *Qualitative Data Analysis: A Sourcebook of New Methods.* Beverly Hills, CA: Sage Publications.

Morgan, A. R., E. Taylor, and E. Gibbs. 1982. Variations in students' approaches to studying. *British Journal of Educational Technology* 13(2):107–113.

Morrison, T. R. 1989. Beyond legitimacy: Facing the future in distance education. *International Journal of Lifelong Education* 8(1):3–24.

Olgren, C. H. 1992. Adults' learning strategies and outcomes in an independent study course. Ph.D. diss., University of Wisconsin-Madison, Madison, WI.

Paul, R. H. 1990. *Open Learning and Open Management: Leadership and Integrity in Distance Education.* London: Kogan Page.

Pintrich, P. R. 1988. A process-oriented view of student motivation and cognition. In *Improving Teaching and Learning Through Research*, eds. J. S. Sork and L. A. Mets. New Directions for Institutional Research. 57:65–79. San Francisco, CA: Jossey-Bass.

Pintrich, P. R., and G. R. Johnson. 1990. Assessing and improving students' learning strategies. In *The Changing Face of College Teaching.* ed., M. D. Svinicki. New Directions for Teaching and Learning, 42:83–92.

Pressley, M., J. G. Borkowski, and W. Schneider. 1987. Cognitive strategies: Good strategy users coordinate megacognition and knowledge. *Annals of Child Development* 4:89–129.

Ramsden, P. D. Beswick, and J. Bowden. 1987. Learning processes and learning skills. In *Student Learning: Research in Education and Cognitive Psychology,* eds. J. Richardson, M. Eysenck, and D. Piper, 168–176. Milton Keynes: Open University Press.

Rhys, S. 1988. Study skills and personal development. *Open Learning* (June):40–42. June.

Shuell, T. J. 1986. Cognitive conceptions of learning. *Review of Educational Research* 56(4):411–436.

Strang, A. 1987. The hidden barriers. In *Beyond Distance Teaching Towards Open Learning,* eds. V. E. Hodgson, S. J. Mann, and R. S. Snell, 26–39. Milton Keynes: Open University Press.

Taylor, E., A. Morgan, and E. Gibbs. 1981. The orientation of Open University foundation students to their studies. *Teaching at a Distance* 20:3–12.

The Cognitive and Technology Group at Vanderbilt. 1993. Anchored instruction and situated cognition revisited. *Educational Technology* 33(3):52–70.

Thomas, J. W., and W. D. Rohwer, Jr. 1986. Academic studying: The role of learning strategies. *Educational Psychologist* 21(1&2):19–41.

Valcke, M. M. A., R. L. Martens, P. H. A. G. Poelmans, and M. M. Daal. 1993. The actual use of embedded support devices in self-study materials by students in a distance education setting. *Distance Education* 14(1):55–84.

Weinstein, C. E., and R. E. Mayer. 1986. The teaching of learning strategies. In *Handbook of Research on Teaching,* 3rd edition, ed. M. C. Wittrock. New York: Macmillan.

3 Examining the Utility of Efficacy Measures in Distance Education Research

Roger Bruning

Introduction

Recent years have brought a resurgence of interest in the self-referential beliefs individuals hold and in the role these beliefs play in their thoughts and actions. No set of beliefs has attracted more attention than self-efficacy, the degree to which individuals consider themselves capable of performing a particular activity (Bandura 1982, 1986, 1993). Self-efficacy, in contrast to the more global construct of self-concept, is task-related. An individual may have high self-efficacy for conversing in French, raising orchids, and doing advanced mathematics, for example, but have low efficacy for selling used cars, making home repairs, and conducting a research study. Self-efficacy is linked to actual performance capabilities, but has functions that go well beyond its being a simple artifact of performance.

Self-efficacy beliefs provide a generative mechanism through which people integrate and apply their existing cognitive, behavioral, and social skills to a task. They also are an important determinant of an individual's decisions about whether or not to engage in particular activities, to put forth effort on a task, and to persevere under conditions of failure. Accomplishment in any area thus not only is built on a set of skills, but also on beliefs that one can use them well (Bandura 1993).

In general, individuals with higher self-efficacy (e.g., who have confidence in themselves as writers, bridge players, or public speakers) will show a number of desirable characteristics in their behavior and outlook, including setting high personal goals in the area of efficacy, using more analytic problem-solving strategies, and persisting rather than ceasing activity under difficult conditions. For highly efficacious persons, new situations tend to be seen as opportunities for achievement. Physiological arousal is interpreted as motivating. In contrast, low efficacious persons tend to set lower goals, to be less flexible in problem solving, and to give up rapidly after failure. In persons with lower efficacy, the physiological arousal generated by unfamiliar performance situations tends to arouse anxiety, which often is interpreted as evidence of inability to perform. Self-efficacy beliefs thus act both as gatekeepers, as individuals select themselves into and out of certain activities based on their beliefs, and as guides for behavior, as individuals variously increase, alter, or cease their efforts based on their beliefs about their capabilities.

Positive efficacy beliefs develop in a variety of ways. Probably the most straightforward and potent route to their development is what Bandura has called enactive mastery, where efficacy builds as a result of feedback from accomplishments, as obstacles are overcome successfully with effort. Another route to higher efficacy is vicarious experience, observing models succeed or not succeed at activities. Seeing a person perform a task permits a comparison of individuals' skills with those of the performer and allows them to decide the potential for success if they attempt the task themselves. Verbal or social persuasion also can build efficacy. Through others' encouragement, confidence grows as individuals are urged to greater effort or coached to attempt approximations of the final performance. Finally, efficacy can be built through positive interpretation of emotional arousal, as factors such as reduced stress, increased stamina, and excitement are given a favorable interpretation.

Given the obvious link between individuals' behaviors in a domain and the beliefs they have about the adequacy of their performance, and the potency of enactive mastery in building efficacy, it perhaps is no surprise that research has shown that self-efficacy ratings correlate consistently with a number of dimensions of actual performance, such as general academic achievement (Schunk 1984), reading (Paris and Oka 1986; Shell, Murphy, and Bruning 1989; Shell, Colvin, and Bruning 1995), writing (Shell, Murphy, and Bruning 1989; Shell, Colvin, and Bruning 1995), and mathematics (Pajares and Miller 1994). This relationship was the basis for the research described in the present paper, which involved using efficacy measures to complement performance measures in evaluating a television-based distance education program. The present study examines the potential utility of these measures in evaluating distance learning programs.

The Distance Learning Program

The Nebraska/SERC Japanese language course is a satellite-based course undertaken by the Nebraska Department of Education, Nebraska Educational Television, and the Satellite Educational Resources Consortium (SERC). Nebraska/SERC Japanese courses were first begun in 1989-90 and since that time have served several thousand students nationally. During the three-year period of our evaluation, as now, the instructional model of this course involved live satellite transmissions three days a week, with instruction conducted in Japanese and supported with a wide assortment of visual aids, props, and skits that provided a context for language learning. During each transmission, students participated live and interactively (one-way video/two-way audio). A key provision of the Nebraska/SERC Japanese I courses was students' opportunity to talk with native speakers via an audio teleconferncing twice a week to practice their newly-learned skills. The native speakers participated in several sessions a day, with a typical session involving students from several schools in different parts of the country.

Evaluation of the Japanese I Course

Because of considerable interest in the Nebraska/SERC Japanese course and because there are widely different views about the effectiveness of foreign language instruction delivered through distance learning methods, we began early on to seek ways of testing the effectiveness of distance language instruction in developing Japanese language skills. One of our major evaluation initiatives involved attempting to compare outcomes in the Nebraska/SERC course with those in conventional courses. Working through state departments of education, we first attempted to locate the regularly offered Japanese I courses in the more than twenty states served by SERC. We then solicited instructors' course outlines and objectives and identified those objectives common to the Nebraska/SERC course and the conventionally-taught courses. These shared objectives were used to develop a test blueprint to create a two-part fifty-item test measuring outcomes in listening (twenty items) and reading (thirty items). This test was first administered to students in SERC and comparison schools in 1990; a second, slightly longer test (sixty items), constructed to the same set of specifications, was administered to a new group of SERC and comparison students at the conclusion of the 1990-91 year. In both years, these measures showed significant differences favoring the SERC group when compared with conventional courses.

While the higher performance of the Nebraska/SERC students on tests composed of items common to both distance learning and traditional instruction gave cause for optimism to the course designers, several alternative explanations were possible. For instance, motivation to perform well in the course and especially to do well on the exam may have differed. School and student selection may have varied in the two groups because of non-random selection. We thus began a search for other measures that would help us begin to rule out these factors in our 1992 evaluation.

We assumed, based on previous research, that self-efficacy ratings should provide an index that correlated with performance. That is, given the previously-documented relationships between self-efficacy beliefs and actual performance in areas ranging from public speaking to mathematics to spelling, we thought it likely that self-efficacy judgments about Japanese language competence should relate to actual measures of Japanese language performance. We further judged that these measures could prove useful in our evaluation because, although they are related to performance, they likely are subject to a different set of contingencies that make them at least partially independent of performance and thus useful for evaluation purposes. For example, test performance might be expected to vary depending on motivation to perform well on the test, with motivation higher in the SERC group. In the case of efficacy judgments, however, there seemed much less reason to expect, *a priori,* that the distance learning group, in contrast to the comparison group, might "fake good" in estimating their competence. If anything, given the greater stake of traditional classroom teachers in their students' performance, the students in the traditional classes might be expected to rate their competency more highly or at least not less favorably than in the distance learning class. Similarly, on ratings of how well they liked their Japanese I class, students in traditional classes might be expected to rate their classes no less favorably, simply because they were rating their own teacher as they rated their liking for the class and were giving these ratings to this person. A final set of measures to help us develop a stronger logic for comparing evaluation outcomes in distance learning and comparison classes were self-reports of student grades, which served as an indicator of overall school achievement. Self-reported grades have been shown in earlier studies to correlate very highly with actual grades. Thus, we proposed to use these grades to help us equate student ability between the distance learning and comparison groups.

The overall results for the 1992 evaluation showed that both test performance and efficacy judgments differed significantly between the distance learning and comparison groups, with differences favoring the distance learning group. As shown in Table 1, these differences were present both for students who previously had taken another foreign language and those who had not. Differences also were present in students of varying overall school achievement, grouped by self-reported grade point average. Further, higher ratings were associated with higher student ratings of course enjoyment by distance learning students and with their greater inclination to recommend the course to their fellow students. Taken together, these data made it possible for us to offer somewhat more secure judgments about whether observed differences in test performance were valid indicators of Japanese language competency.

Table 1. Total Achievement Test Scores and Self-efficacy Ratings for Students Who Had and Who Had Not Previously Studied a Foreign Language

Measure	Distance Learning		Comparison	
	Mean	SD	Mean	SD
Students for Whom Japanese Was First Foreign Language				
Achievement	43.21	11.86	31.87	10.15
Efficacy	76.83	16.49	61.67	17.84
Students Who Previously Had Studied Another Foreign Language				
Achievement	46.21	10.66	31.55	9.41
Efficacy	80.49	14.54	62.25	18.65

Note. Data are from Table 4 in Bruning, et al. (1993, 35). Students categorized as previously having studied a foreign language are those students who reported at least one year of foreign language study.

A Closer Examination of Efficacy Measures

The present paper is directed toward a closer scrutiny of the efficacy measures and their functioning. The results that follow, therefore, further examine these measures and the nature of their relationships to other measures. Table 2 presents the efficacy items and mean ratings on each of the items in the distance learning and comparison groups. As is typically done in measures of efficacy, individuals rated the probability that they could perform these behaviors on a scale from 0 to 100. The first five items required estimates of competency in areas likely to be covered in most Japanese I courses, such as greetings, counting, and telling time. The second set of five items, in contrast, were designed to elicit judgments about whether the students *someday* saw themselves attaining the level of competency entailed by each item. Thus, these were not, strictly speaking, efficacy judgments, but are closely related to the efficacy construct. For the set of items measuring judgments about current performance (SE-I), Cronbach's alpha was eighty-eight. For the second set of items (SE-II), those eliciting estimates of confidence about attaining future goals related to Japanese language study, Cronbach's alpha was ninety-three.

Table 2. Efficacy Ratings on Individual Items for Japanese Language Use by Japanese I Students (Ratings are 0 to 100 percent confidence)

	Distance Learning		Comparison	
	Mean	SD	Mean	SD
RATE YOUR CONFIDENCE (0-100%) IN BEING ABLE TO DO EACH OF THESE NOW				
Give directions in Japanese to a driver	48.7	31.5	20.7	26.7
Make a brief phone call in Japanese	67.5	30.2	29.6	30.8
Greet another person in Japanese	91.4	21.4	68.6	38.0
Count to 100 in Japanese	76.7	31.6	59.7	40.7
Tell time in Japanese	82.3	28.4	47.0	40.7
RATE YOUR CONFIDENCE (0-100%) THAT YOU COULD DO THESE SOMEDAY				
Master Japanese well enough to get along on a trip to Japan	68.1	33.5	45.2	39.7
Read letters in Japanese from a Japanese pen pal	68.6	32.2	53.6	39.3
Attend a school or college in Japan	42.4	34.7	29.9	33.5
Converse in Japanese with a visitor from Japan	64.7	32.5	50.2	45.0
Read Japanese newspapers or magazines	55.9	33.6	45.5	40.5

Note. N in distance learning group was 1219. N in the comparison group was 753.

The scales were, in fact, strongly related to each another, with a correlation of .71 between total ratings on the first and the second scales for the combined group. Principal components analysis of the ten items showed all items loading quite strongly (above .7) on one factor (eigenvalue = 6.30), which accounted for 63% of the total variance, but with a second factor present that accounted for approximately 11% of the variance (eigenvalue = 1.10). A varimax rotation showed the items to sort themselves into two groups corresponding to the "present" and "future" clusters, with all items loading above .70 on its factor.

Table 3 presents the correlations between the individual items and performance on the test segments for the distance learning and comparison groups. As can be seen, correlations between the efficacy measures and listening and reading performance were relatively high, as expected, in the distance learning group. Correlations of efficacy judgments with overall grades (last column), in contrast, were relatively small, an expected finding since efficacy judgments should be largely domain-specific. That is, they typically relate more strongly to the area of performance under consideration than to general ability factors.

The comparison group, however, produced a pattern of relationships in which efficacy judgments shared much less variance with the performance measures than in the distance learning group. Also in contrast to the distance learning group, students in the comparison group who had higher grades tended to have lower efficacy judgments. Further analyses were undertaken to examine these differences.

Table 3. Relationship Betweeen Japanese Language Performance Measures, Summed Efficacy Measures, and Grades in Distance Learning and Comparison Groups in Japanese I

| | Performance Measures | | Efficacy Measures | | |
	Listening	Reading	SE-I	SE-II	Grades
Distance Learning Group ($N = 1219$)					
Listening	1.00	.74	.44	.36	.31
Reading		1.00	.46	.39	.37
SE-I			1.00	.63	.14
SE-II				1.00	.14
Grades					1.00
Comparison Group ($N = 753$)					
Listening	1.00	.50	.17	.16	.22
Reading		1.00	.15	.17	.27
SE-I			1.00	.66	-.28
SE-II				1.00	-.16
Grades					1.00

Note. Listening and Reading are subtest scores on Japanese I test. SE-I is the average of judgments on the first five efficacy items (the "present" items) and SE-II the average on the second five items (the "future" items).

Table 4 presents the relationships between the individual efficacy items with test performance and grades for the distance learning group and the comparison group. As can be seen, for the distance learning group, ratings on virtually all of the efficacy items were related to performance on the listening and reading portions of the test, with generally low relationships to overall classroom performance, as indicated by self-reported grades. The analyses for the comparison group, however, revealed generally low observed relationships between efficacy judgments about Japanese language competency and actual measured performance.

Table 4. Relationships Between Specific Efficacy Judgments, Japanese Language Performance Measures, and Grades in Distance Learning and Comparison Groups in Japanese I

Efficacy Judgment	Distance Learning			Comparison		
	Listen	Read	Grades	Listen	Read	Grades
RATE YOUR CONFIDENCE (0-100%) IN BEING ABLE TO DO EACH OF THESE NOW						
Give directions in Japanese . . .	.39	.40	.15	.16	.13	-.10
To make a brief phone call . . .	.34	.34	.11	.13	.12	-.14
Greet another person . . .	.19	.21	-.06	.02	.02	-.13
Count to 100 . . .	.40	.42	.18	.18	.15	-.37
Tell time . . .	.39	.41	.13	.15	.15	-.20
RATE YOUR CONFIDENCE (0-100%) THAT YOU COULD DO THESE SOMEDAY						
Get along on a trip to Japan . . .	.33	.36	.13	.13	.13	-.19
Read letters from pen pal . . .	.31	.34	.10	.10	.12	-.16
Attend college in Japan . . .	.28	.34	.13	.12	.19	-.06
Talk with a visitor . . .	.34	.36	.13	.09	.13	-.11
Read Japanese newspapers . . .	.32	.34	.11	.24	.18	-.15

Regression analyses examining total test performance as a function of ability and belief variables were conducted separately for the distance learning and comparison groups. To examine the effects of efficacy and other belief measures independent of general ability, self-reported grades were initially forced into the regression analysis, followed by stepwise analysis of the remaining variables, which included the two efficacy judgments, liking for the course, and outcome expectancies for the course. In the distance learning group, R^2 with self-reported grades entered was .13 (F = 185.41, p < .001); in the comparison group R^2 was .08 (F = 67.85, p < .001). With the effect of grades removed, significant variables for the distance learning group were SE-I (R^2 change = .34, F = 329.78, p < .001) and liking for the course (R^2 change = .02, F = 37.81, p < .001). SE-II and outcome expectancies for the course did not enter the equation. The final multiple regression of .58 accounted for more than a third of the variance in test performance. In the comparison group, with the effects of grades removed, significant variables were SE-I (R^2 change = .16, F = 70.94, p < .001), outcome expectancies for the course (R^2 change = .005, F = 4.57, p < .05), and SE-II (R^2 change = .007, F = 6.91, p < .01). The final multiple regression of .42 in the comparison group accounted for about 17% of the variation in test performance.

As was seen earlier, the distance learning group overall scored consistently higher on measures of actual Japanese listening and reading performance than did the comparison group and rated their efficacy higher. To permit closer examination of the relationships between efficacy and performance in the two groups, each group was divided into subgroups of students who reported higher and lower overall grades in school. The higher groups in the distance learning and comparison groups consisted of students who reported their grades as As or As and Bs, while the lower group consisted of students who reported that their grades were mostly Bs, Bs and Cs, or Cs and below. In the distance learning group, as expected, the students reporting better grades outperformed those with lower reported grades (Listening$_{higher}$ D = 20.94 vs. Listening$_{lower}$ D = 17.75; Reading$_{higher}$ D = 26.64 vs. Reading$_{lower}$ D = 21.08). Corresponding to their performance, students with better overall grades rated their efficacy an average of approximately 10 percentage points higher than did students in the lower group (SE-I$_{higher}$ D = 76.5 vs. SE-I$_{lower}$ D = 66.3; SE-II$_{higher}$ D = 63.3 vs. SE-II$_{lower}$ D = 52.5). In the comparison group, however, efficacy ratings did not correspond closely with actual performance. While the test performance of the comparison group students with higher self-reported grades was significantly higher than that of their counterparts who reported lower grades (Listening$_{higher}$ C = 15.90 vs. Listening$_{lower}$ C = 12.97; Reading$_{higher}$ C = 18.41 vs. Reading$_{lower}$ C = 14.99), their efficacy judgments actually were lower in the group reporting higher grades (SE-I$_{higher}$ C = 43.2 vs. SE-I$_{lower}$ C = 48.7; SE-II $_{higher}$ C = 46.6 vs. SE-II$_{lower}$ C = 46.7).

Table 5 shows correlations between efficacy judgments and actual measures for the students reporting higher and lower overall school grades in the distance learning and comparison groups. As can be seen, consistent relationships between efficacy were present between efficacy ratings and performance in both higher and lower ability distance learning groups. In the comparison group, however, relationships between efficacy and actual performance were much lower in the group with higher grades than in the group with lower grades.

Table 5. Relationships Between Japanese Language Performance Measures, Summed Efficacy Measures, and for Students with Reported Lower and Higher Overall School Grades in Distance Learning and Comparison Groups

	Listening	Reading	SE-I	SE-II
Distance Learning Group				
Distance Learning Students with Lower School Grades (N = 382)				
Listening	1.00	.72	.43	.34
Reading		1.00	.43	.38
SE-I			1.00	.63
SE-II				1.00
Distance Learning Students with Higher School Grades (N = 837)				
Listening	1.00	.70	.39	.31
Reading		1.00	.41	.35
SE-I			1.00	.70
SE-II				1.00
Comparison Group				
Comparison Group Students with Lower School Grades (N = 263)				
Listening	1.00	.31	.34	.23
Reading		1.00	.31	.27
SE-I			1.00	.53
SE-II				1.00
Comparison Group Students with Higher School Grades (N = 490)				
Listening	1.00	.53	.15	.13
Reading		1.00	.14	.14
SE-I			1.00	.71
SE-II				1.00

Note. Listening and Reading are subtest scores on Japanese I test. SE-I is the average of judgments on the first five efficacy items (the "present" items) and SE-II the average on the second five items (the "future" items).

Discussion

The present study examined the utility of efficacy judgments as a potential source of evaluative information complementary to that provided by performance measures. In general, the results are positive. The present data clearly show that efficacy ratings are associated with actual performance and do contribute additional information about the likelihood of skilled performance in a particular content domain. In both groups, self-efficacy accounted for a significant portion of the variance in Japanese language test performance, independent of the effect of students' general level of performance in school. They also served as a metric of student beliefs about their abilities in Japanese. For example, efficacy judgments provided information that students in the distance learning class were highly confident in their ability to perform oral language skills of greeting other people in Japanese, telling time, and counting. The "future" items also were a source of useful evaluative information, revealing a high degree of expectation in these students that they expected to be able to communicate in significant ways with Japanese-speaking people through conversation and reading. Coupled with positive ratings of the course and a higher level of willingness of the students in the distance learning class to recommend the course to others, the general picture conveyed about this distance learning class is a remarkably positive one. In contrast, Japanese I students in the comparison group were much less confident in their abilities and also much less optimistic about achieving higher levels of performance in using Japanese; these results are consistent with lower patterns of test performance and lower ratings of affective dimensions of their classes.

From the standpoint of evaluation methodology, efficacy ratings appear to be a useful tool to give evaluators additional information about the overall utility of a distance learning program. Accomplishment in any area of performance involves not only the set of skills that participants are developing, but also the beliefs that they are capable of using the skills and their willingness to deploy them. These beliefs, as Bandura and many others have shown repeatedly (e.g., see Bandura 1993), are significant factors in individuals' decisions about whether or not to undertake tasks, to work toward achievement in the task area, and to continue on when failure is encountered. The importance of these relationships should not be underestimated. In the present language learning setting, for instance, one would expect that efficacy beliefs would lie on the causal path to decisions about whether to continue study of Japanese, how hard and persistently to work at mastering a language many find difficult, and how students responded to difficulties ranging from a lost textbook to failure on an examination.

A somewhat puzzling aspect of the present data is the lower-than-expected relationship of efficacy judgments to test performance observed in the comparison group, coupled with the low negative relationship of Japanese language efficacy with school grades. For instance, whereas correlations in the distance learning group of individual efficacy items with test segments ranged from +.19 to .42 (median = .34), correlations in the comparison group of efficacy items with test segments ranged from near zero only up to .24 (median = .13). In contrast to the expected low positive correlations of the Japanese language efficacy with overall school grades, such as that observed in the distance learning group, the correlations of these same items with grades in the comparison group, although low, were consistently negative, ranging from -.06 to -.37 (median r = -.14). The findings for the comparison group thus are somewhat inconsistent both with theoretical predictions and with empirical findings from earlier studies.

To some extent, these findings may underscore the domain-specific nature of efficacy judgments. While we worked from common areas of course outlines in constructing both test and efficacy measures, the areas of judged efficacy, which focused on oral language use, may not have mapped as well on the course experiences of students in the comparison classrooms. Traditional language instruction has emphasized reading and grammatical analyses, which the efficacy judgments did not tap extensively. Also, the results in Table 5 show that the main source for the lower-than-expected relationship of efficacy to performance in the comparison group was the upper-ability students. It may be that upper-ability students, who along with many of their fellow students in the comparison group did not do particularly well on the examination, might have been particularly discouraged by their relatively low performance (Bandura and Cervone 1983). That is, their efficacy, in contrast to that of their less able peers, may have been significantly lowered by performance that, for them, was unexpectedly low. Further study is needed to explore learners' responses to efficacy measures and the relationship of these measures to performance under a variety of conditions, including degree of expectation of success as it relates to actual performance.

References

Bandura, A. 1982. Self-efficacy mechanisms in human agency. *American Psychologist* 37:122–147.

Bandura, A. 1986. *Social Foundations of Thought and Action: A Social Cognitive Theory.* Englewood Cliffs, NJ: Prentice-Hall.

Bandura, A. 1993. Perceived self-efficacy in cognitive development and functioning. *Educational Psychologist* 28:117–148.

Bandura, A., and D. Cervone. 1983. Self-evaluative and self-efficacy mechanisms governing the motivational effects of goal systems. *Journal of Personality and Social Psychology* 45:1017–1028.

Bruning, R., M. Landis, E. Hoffman, and K. Grosskopf. 1993. Perspectives on an interactive satellite-based Japanese language course. *The American Journal of Distance Education* 7:22–38.

Pajares, F., and D. Miller. 1994. Role of self-efficacy and self-concept beliefs in mathematical problem solving: A path analysis. *Journal of Educational Psychology* 86:193–203.

Paris, S. G., and R. Oka. 1986. Children's reading strategies, metacognition and motivation. *Developmental Review* 6:25–56.

Shell, D., C. Murphy, and R. Bruning. 1989. Self-efficacy and outcome expectancy mechanisms in reading and writing achievement. *Journal of Educational Psychology* 81:91–100.

Shell, D., C. Colvin, and R. Bruning. 1995. Developmental and ability differences in self-efficacy, causal attribution, and outcome expectancy mechanisms in reading and writing achievement. *Journal of Educational Psychology* 87:386–398.

Schunk, D. 1984. Self-efficacy perspective on achievement behavior. *Educational Psychologist* 19:848–857.

4   The Loneliness of the Long Distance Learner

Rudy Pugliese

Introduction

As a teacher and researcher of human and mediated communication, I have wondered what would be the effect of eliminating or minimizing interpersonal contact in education. Yet this is exactly what separates distance education from traditional face-to-face instruction. Could the lack of interpersonal interaction result in feelings of loneliness? Might these feelings affect a student's ability to achieve academically? Is loneliness a lack of interpersonal interaction or does it include group affiliation? In short, does loneliness constitute a problem for the distance learner?

Although loneliness was rarely professionally investigated until the 1970s (Peplau and Perlman 1982a), research on and concern with loneliness has increased in the last decade (McWhirter 1990). Perlman (1987) suggests five reasons for the growth of research: a) documentation that loneliness was widespread and could undermine well-being, b) a general increase in interest in relationships, c) a psychometrically sound scale became available (the UCLA Loneliness Scale), d) a cooperative network of scholars secured special funding, and e) researchers began using innovative and sophisticated methods.

Loneliness Defined

Although there is agreement that loneliness concerns a dissatisfaction with the state of one's interpersonal relationships, researchers differ on how to define the construct of loneliness. Weiss (1973) defines loneliness as "a response to an unfulfilled need for a relationship or set of relationships" (p. 17). The author also distinguishes between social and emotional loneliness. The former is due to a lack of community ties while the latter is due to a lack of intimate others. Peplau and Perlman (1982b) define it as the "extent to which a person's network of social relationships is smaller or less satisfying than the person desires" (p. 2). Similarly, Spitzberg (1981) defines loneliness as the "state of dissatisfaction with the achieved versus desired relational intimacy" (p. 2).

Loneliness and Adjustment to College

Although loneliness affects all segments of society, college students are especially vulnerable (Jones 1982; Russell 1982). According to Cutrona (1982) 75% of college freshman reported having experienced loneliness since beginning school. Over 40% rated their loneliness moderate to severe in intensity. Chronically lonely students attributed their loneliness to enduring traits while the transiently lonely faulted a wide range of situational and dispositional factors. Situational factors cited by students included leaving family and friends (40%), the breakup of a romantic relationship (15%), problems with a friend or roommate (11%), difficulties with schoolwork (11%), and family problems (9%).

Russell, Peplau, and Cutrona (1980) report that lonely students spend more time alone, date less, eat alone more often, and spend more weekend evenings alone than their friends. They have significantly lower self esteem, are more introverted, have lower affiliative tendencies, are less assertive, and are more sensitive to rejection. Goswick and Jones (1981) found that loneliness was negatively related to social facility, regularity, approval, and involvement and positively related to alienation, parental disinterest, negative school attitudes, and feelings of inferiority.

Loneliness and Academic Achievement

A number of studies have reported that loneliness affects academic performance, but the results are inconsistent. Rubin (1979) reports that loneliness is negatively related to grade point average. Booth (1983) investigated the relationship between college grade point average (GPA), composite American College Test (ACT) scores, intelligence quotient (IQ), and gender to loneliness. Males were significantly more lonely than females, and females' loneliness correlated negatively with the ACT, GPA, and IQ. In contrast Ponzetti and Cate (1981) found that loneliness and academic performance, as measured by grade point averages, were negatively related for males but unrelated for females.

Students who fail to develop satisfying interpersonal relationships are less likely to earn good grades and less likely to persist in college (Pace 1970; Tinto

1975). Those who do form supportive relationships have an advantage in that they benefit from shared information regarding school: suggesting courses and professors to take or not to take, editing each others papers, sharing notes, preparing for exams, and helping each other to understand difficult material. Particularly at residential institutions, peer relationships provide emotional support (Shaver, Furman, and Buhrmester 1985). They provide help in coping with problems, relieving stress, sharing successes, and coping with failure. They also allow for social integration and a sense of belonging (Davis and Todd 1985; McAdams 1985). Those who fail to establish meaningful relationships tend not to do as well academically and are more at risk for dropping out (Baker and Siryk 1980). Loneliness has been found to distinguish between persisters and nonpersisters in a residential university (Hawken, Duran, and Kelly 1991) but not in telecourse students in a community college (Pugliese 1994).

Nezlek, Wheeler, and Reis (1990) report gender differences regarding social interaction and academic achievement and indicate that men who are socially integrated may be putting their grades at risk: "...the news, at least for men, is not all that cheerful. The bookworm is probably a better description of the academically successful student than is the BMOC. For women however, academic success seems to have no social cost, the bookworm and BWOC are equally likely descriptors of academically successful females" (p. 308).

Burleson and Samter (1992) challenged that finding by reanalyzing the same data and using Fisher's r to z transformation on the correlations. They found no gender differences in the relationship between academic achievement and social participation. In a second study reported in the same article, the authors observed a significant positive association between loneliness and GPA for males ($r = .25$, $p < .01$) but not for females ($r = .05$, $p < .10$) indicating that lonelier males earned higher grades. However, there were no significant differences in the magnitudes of correlations for males and females between GPA and loneliness as measured by the Revised UCLA Loneliness Scale. Since the authors used a sample of 208 fraternity and sorority members, the results may not generalize to other populations, particularly to distance education students.

The UCLA Loneliness Scale

The most widely used instrument to assess loneliness is the Revised UCLA Loneliness Scale (Paloutzian and Janigan 1987; Russell 1982; Russell, Peplau, and Cutrona 1880; Russell, Peplau, and Furguson 1978). In 1987, Paloutzian and Janigan reported that since 1980, approximately 80% of the journal articles investigating loneliness have used either the original or Revised UCLA Loneliness Scale and that 80% of the subjects were college students. The authors argue that "the majority of the psychological study of loneliness has been primarily a one-scale, one-subject-pool science" (p. 34).

The original 20-item version of the scale was found to have high reliability and validity estimates (Russell, Peplau, and Furguson 1978). Since all of the questions were negatively worded, it was later revised to avoid response bias. The Revised UCLA Loneliness Scale consisted of ten negatively and ten positively worded statements, none of which uses the word "loneliness" (Russell, Peplau, and Cutrona 1980). The authors reported impressive evidence of convergent and discriminant validity.

Factor Analytical Studies

The revised scale is supposed to be unidimensional, yet a number of authors have conducted factor analytic studies and report that the scale is multidimensional.

Hojat (1982) used principal components analysis with a varimax rotation to produce four and five-factor solutions explaining 43% and 43.4% of the variance respectively. Although eigenvalues were above 1.00, the author failed to include criteria for retaining items on a factor. The author concludes that the Scale is multidimensional. The sample was composed of 232 Iranian students attending American universities and 305 Iranian students attending Iranian universities.

Zakahi and Duran (1982) performed a principal-factor analysis with orthogonal rotation and produced a two-factor solution accounting for 40% of the variance. One dimension was labeled "intimate other" and consisted of ten items; the other dimension was labeled "social network" and consisted of the remaining ten items. However, they failed to identify which questions loaded on each factor or their criteria for selection of the factors. The authors used a sample of 287 college students.

Austin (1983) produced a three-factor solution that accounted for 55.6% of the variance using principal-components analysis with varimax rotation. The author specified that a minimum eigenvalue of 1.00 was used with a minimum loading of .40. The three dimensions were labeled "intimate others," "social others," and "belonging and affiliation." All ten negatively-worded items loaded on the factor labeled "intimate others" while the positive items loaded on the dimensions of "social others" and "belonging and affiliation." Austin used a sample of 493 college students enrolled in Liberal Arts classes at Rochester Institute of Technology.

Newcomb and Bentler (1986) produced a one-factor solution but failed to specify their method. Although there were four eigenvalues above 1.00, they noted a large drop between the first and second factors. They conclude the Scale is unidimensional. They used a sample of 739 young adults.

Hays and DiMatteo (1987) factor analyzed the Scale using an oblique Promax rotation. Using Cattell's (1966) scree test and Montanelli and Humphreys' (1976) parallel analysis, five factors were required. Using eight items that loaded on the first factor, the authors suggest a substitute for the 20-item form. Loneliness was not significantly related to satisfaction with teachers in school or satisfaction with school performance, but significantly related to alienation, social anxiety, satisfaction with friends, and satisfaction with self among other variables. Gender differences were reported with males significantly lonelier than females. The authors used a sample of 199 college students.

Adams et al. (1988) performed factor analysis using both varimax and oblique rotations to produce a three-factor solution. They labeled the dimensions "psychological loneliness, "psychosocial loneliness," and "social loneliness." Again the first and third factors consisted of negatively worded items while the second factor consisted of the positively worded items. Five items failed to load highly enough on any of the factors. The authors used a sample of 243 female college students.

Based on a sample of 978 adults in New Zealand, a two-factor solution was reported with the positively worded items loading on one dimension and the negatively worded items loading on the other (Knight et al. 1988). The authors claim that the absence of an "always" alternative resulted in a more pronounced J-shaped distribution of scores on the positive items. They reason that the intercorrelations between positive items or negative items resulted in two factors. They conclude that it is misleading to view the UCLA Loneliness Scale as two dimensional and claim that it is more accurately considered unidimensional.

Mahon and Yarcheski (1990) performed a principal-components analysis with varimax rotation to produce a one-factor solution. Upon further analysis, they produced a five-factor solution. The application of a scree test indicated the superiority of a two-factor solution. The authors conclude that although the loading of positive items on one dimension and negative items on the other might suggest a method artifact, it reflects the bidimensionality of the instrument. The authors labeled the first factor "social network" and the second factor "intimate others." The authors used a sample of 326 seventh and eighth graders. Hartshorne (1993) points out that the negatively-worded items Mahon and Yarcheski call "social network" Austin calls "intimate others," and the positively-worded items they call "intimate others" Austin calls "social others." The author suggests there is confusion regarding the dimensions.

Hartshorne (1993) used a confirmatory factor analysis to test for goodness of fit of various solutions. One-factor, two-factor, and three-factor models were tested. One concern the author voiced is the assumption that Likert-type scales are interval—especially when the scale has fewer than five points. A second concern was the assumption of a normal distribution. One finding was that the revised scale was bimodal. Since it could be due to sampling characteristics, the author suggests that other data samples be examined. The author concludes that the scale is unidimensional but that it is not at all clear if loneliness as a construct is unidimensional or multidimensional. Hartshorne used a sample of 220 college students at a midwestern university.

The diversity of findings on the dimensionality of the scale suggests that the instrument may be measuring a more complex construct than its authors have defined. Although intended to reflect a dissatisfaction with networks or relationships in general, the scale has inadvertently pointed to a distinction in such a way as to describe relationships with more than one person tending to load separately from the questions involving single individuals. Even if one concludes that negatively and positively phrased questions loading on separate factors is a method artifact, the bulk of studies report that at least two dimensions are still left. The loneliness literature has been heavily dependent on traditionally-aged college students in residential institutions. If sampling characteristics are affecting distribution of the scores, perhaps different samples are needed. The present study investigated a sample of telecourse students in a distance education setting.

Method

Subjects. The data reported here are part of an earlier study investigating psychological predictors of persistence/withdrawal behavior (see Pugliese 1994). The subjects were telecourse students enrolled in a community college in the greater New York area in the spring of 1989. Of the 306 participating, 174 were female and 132 were male.

A telephone survey was used to reach students. Of the total 778 students registered for telecourses, 314 were contacted and 306 completed the survey; eight refused to take part.

Survey Instrument and Procedures. The questionnaire included the Revised UCLA Loneliness Scale (Russell, Peplau, and Cutrona 1980), the dyadic apprehension dimension of the Personal Report of Communication Apprehension (McCroskey 1982), the social experience and social confirmation dimension of the Communication Adaptability Scale (Duran 1983), the James Internal-External Locus of Control Scale (Robinson and Shaver 1973), and additional demographic items. Grades were obtained from the registrar.

The Revised UCLA Loneliness Scale response items were changed to include a fifth response to facilitate administering the scale. Since the Communication Adaptability Scale (CAS) is a five-point Likert scale, the response of "always" was added to "often," "sometimes," "rarely," "never." Although not originally intended, the addition might avoid Hartshorne's (1993) concern that Likert-type scales might not be interval when there are fewer than five possible responses.

Results and Discussion. Pearson correlations were used to test for significance. None of the independent variables was significantly related to academic achievement as measured by grade point average (see Table 1). The sample was than divided by gender and correlations were computed. Again, none of the independent variables were significantly related to GPA. Loneliness was also unrelated to age, but grade point average was significantly and positively related to age ($r = .32$, $p = <.01$). Since younger, traditionally-aged students might be more affected by loneliness, correlations were computed for traditionally-aged students (18 to 24-year olds). The relationship between loneliness and grade point average for these students was also nonsignificant.

Table 1. Correlation Coefficients

Grade Point Average (for both genders)

Loneliness	-.10
Social Experience	.04
Social Confirmation	.04
Dyadic Apprehension	-.01
Locus of Control	-.04

Grade Point Average

	Men	Women
Loneliness	-.10	-.06

Age

Loneliness	.01

Grade Point Average

Age	.32**

Grade Point Average
(18 to 24-year olds)

Loneliness	-.07

** Significant < .01

Factor analysis was performed on student responses to the Revised UCLA loneliness Scale using SPSS-X (Statistical Package for the Social Sciences 1988). A principal components analysis using an orthogonal (varimax) rotation was employed (See Table 2). The analysis produced a four-factor solution with eigenvalues greater than 1.00 accounting for 57.4% of the variance and converging in ten iterations. Factor loadings of .40 or greater were required. If one were to apply Gorsuch's (1983) criterion, and eliminate rotated factors consisting of only two or three items loading .30 or higher, the fourth factor, social isolation, would be considered trivial.

Table 2. Factorial Solution for the Revised UCLA Loneliness Scale

Items	Loading
Factor 1: Lack of Intimate Others	
I lack companionship.	.62
There is no one I can turn to.	.65
I do not feel alone.	.63
I am no longer close to anyone.	.70
I feel left out.	.60
No one really knows me well.	.48
I feel isolated from others.	.55
I am unhappy being so withdrawn.	.64
Factor 2: Intimate Others	
There are people I feel close to.	.57
I can find companionship when I want it.	.70
There are people who really understand me.	.52
There are people I can talk to.	.85
There are people I can turn to.	.88
Factor 3: Social Integration	
I feel in tune with the people around me.	.54
I feel part of a group of friends.	.61
I have a lot in common with the people around me.	.68
I am an outgoing person.	.64
Factor 4: Social Isolation	
My interests and ideas are not shared by those around me.	.59
My social relationships are superficial.	.70
People are around me but not with me.	.48

Nonetheless, there are still three factors, with the negatively stated items loading on the first factor. The first factor had an eigenvalue of 7.76 and explained 38.8 percent of the variance. The second factor had an eigenvalue of 1.4 and explained 7.1 percent of the variance. The third factor had an eigenvalue of 1.25 and explained 6.3% of the variance. If negatively and positively stated items loading separately indicates a method artifact, the two dimensions clearly show a difference between the need for one other person and the need for people. Although the Revised UCLA Loneliness Scale was intended to be unidimensional, the bulk of factor analytical studies indicates it is multidimensional. Consequently, the construct of loneliness might be modified to include the lack of social others as well as intimate others. Future researchers might investigate lonliness as a two-dimensional variable.

However one defines loneliness, it does not appear that it or any of the measures of social skills has affected academic achievement in this study. It may be that the interpersonal dimension in mediated education is not only lacking but unrelated to academic achievement. One explanation might be that the diminished social expectations students have in a telecourse result in greater concentration on academic matters. Another might be that the lack of interaction minimizes the bias instructors might have toward the more socially skilled.

In sum, loneliness does not constitute a problem for distance learners if one is solely concerned with course completion and grades. However, if one is concerned with the quality of the learning experience, loneliness may relate to feelings of satisfaction or dissatisfaction. Since one characteristic of distance education is the separation of the learner from the teachers and other learners, perhaps loneliness may explain or predict problems learners may have with other aspects of their educational experience. Alumni giving, school spirit, post-graduation satisfaction, public relations, future enrollment are all potential effects and area of future investigation.

References

Adams, G. R., D. K. Openshaw, L. Bennion, T. Mills, and S. Noble. 1988. Loneliness in late adolescence. *Journal of Adolescent Research* 3:81–96.

Austin, B. A. 1983. Factorial structure of the UCLA Loneliness Scale. *Psychological Reports* 53:883–889.

Baker, R., and B. Siryk. 1980. Alienation and freshman transition in college. *Journal of College Student Personnel* 21:437–442.

Booth, R. 1983. An examination of college GPA, composite ACT scores, IQs, and gender in relation to loneliness of college students. *Psychological Reports* 53:347–352.

Burleson, B. R., and W. Samter. 1992. Are there gender differences in the relationship between academic performance and social behavior? *Human Communication Research* 19:155–175.

Cattell, R. B. 1966. The scree test for the number of factors. *Multivariate Behavioral Research* 1:245–276.

Cutrona, C. E. 1982. Transition to college: Loneliness and the process of social adjustment. In *Loneliness: A Sourcebook of Current Research, Theory, and Therapy,* eds. L. A. Peplau and D. Perlman, 291–309. New York: Wiley and Sons.

Davis, K. E., and M. J. Todd. 1985. Assessing friendship: Prototypes, paradigm cases, and relationship description. In *Understanding Personal Relationships,* eds. S. Duck and D. Perlman, 17–38. London: Sage.

Duran, R. L. 1983. Communicative adaptability: A measure of social communicative competence. *Communication Quarterly* 31:320–326.

Gorsuch, R. L. 1983. *Factor Analysis.* Hillside, NJ: Lawrence Erlbaum Associates.

Goswick, R. A., and W. H. Jones. 1981. Loneliness, self concept, and adjustment. *Journal of Psychology* 107:237–240.

Hartshorne, T. S. 1993. Psychometric properties and confirmatory factor analysis of the UCLA Loneliness Scale. *Journal of Personality Assessment* 61:182–195.

Hawken, L., R. L. Duran, and L. Kelly. 1991. The relationship of interpersonal communication variables to academic success and persistence in college. *Communication Quarterly* 39:297–308.

Hays, R. D., and M. R. DiMatteo. 1987. A short-form measure of loneliness. *Journal of Personality Assessment* 51:69–81.

Hojat, M. 1982. Psychometric characteristics of the UCLA Loneliness Scale: A study with Iranian college students. *Educational and Psychological Measurement* 42:917–925.

Jones, W. H. 1982. Loneliness and social behavior. In *Loneliness: A Sourcebook of Current Theory, Research, and Therapy*, eds. L. A. Peplau and D. Perlman, 238–254. New York: Wiley.

Knight, R. G., B. J. Chisholm, N. G. Marsh, and H. P. D. Godfrey. 1988. Some normative, reliability, and factor analytic data for the revised UCLA Loneliness Scale. *Journal of Clinical Psychology* 44:203–206.

Mahon, N. E., and A. Yarcheski. 1990. The dimensionality of the UCLA Loneliness Scale. *Research in Nursing and Health* 13:45–52.

McAdams, D. P. 1985. Motivation in friendship. In *Understanding Personal Relationships*, eds. S. Duck and D. Perlman, 85–106. London: Sage.

McCroskey, J. C. (1982). *An Introduction to Rhetorical Communication.* 4th ed. Englewood Cliffs, NJ: Prentice-Hall.

McWhirter, B. T. 1990. Loneliness: A review of current literature, with implications for counseling and research. *Journal of Counseling and Development* 68:417–422.

Montanelli, R. G., and L. G. Humphreys. 1976. Latent roots of random data correlation matrices with squared multiple correlations on the diagonal: A Monte Carlo study. *Psychometrica* 41:341–348.

Newcomb, M. D., and P. M. Bentler. 1986. Loneliness and social support: A confirmatory hierarchical analysis. *Personality and Social Psychology Bulletin* 12:520–535.

Nezlek, J. B., L. Wheeler, and H. Reis. 1990. Academic performance and social behavior. *Journal of Performance and Social Behavior* 11:291–309.

Pace, T. 1970. Roommate dissatisfaction in residence halls. *Journal of College Student Personnel* 11:144–147.

Paloutzian, R. F., and A. S. Janigan. 1987. Models and methods in loneliness research: Their status and direction. Special issue: Loneliness: Theory, research, and applications. *Journal of Social Behavior and Personality* 2:31–36.

Peplau, L. A. and D. Perlman. 1982a. *Loneliness: A Sourcebook of Current Theory, Research, and Therapy*. New York: Wiley and Sons.

Peplau, L. A., and D. Perlman. 1982b. Perspectives on loneliness. In *Loneliness: A Sourcebook of Current Theory, Research, and Therapy*, eds. L. A. Peplau and D. Perlman, 1–20. New York: Wiley & Sons.

Perlman, D. 1987. Further reflections on the present state of loneliness research. Special issue: Loneliness: Theory, research, and applications. *Journal of Social Behavior and Personality* 2:17–26.

Ponzetti, J. J., and R. M. Cate. 1981. Sex differences in the relationship between loneliness and academic performance. *Psychological Reports* 48:758.

Pugliese, R. 1994. Telecourse persistence and psychological variables. *The American Journal of Distance Education* 8(3):22–39.

Robinson, J. P., and P. R. Shaver. 1973. *Measures of Social Psychological Attitudes*. Ann Arbor, MI: Survey Research Center Institute for Social Research.

Rubin, A. 1979. Seeking a cure for loneliness. *Psychology Today* 14:82–90.

Russell, D. A. 1982. The measurement of loneliness. In *Loneliness: A Sourcebook of Current Theory, Research, and Therapy*, eds. L. A. Peplau and D. Perlman, 81–104. New York: Wiley & Sons.

Russell, D. A., L. A. Peplau, and Cutrona, C. E. 1980. The revised UCLA Loneliness Scale: Concurrent and discriminant validity evidence. *Journal of Personality and Social Psychology* 39:472–480.

Russell, D. A., L. A. Peplau, and M. L. Furguson.1978. Developing a measure of loneliness. *Journal of Personality Assessment* 42:290–294.

Shaver, P., W. Furman, and D. Buhrmester. 1985. Transition to college: Network changes, social skills, and loneliness. In *Understanding Personal Relationships*, eds. S. Duck and D. Perlman, 193–219. London: Sage.

Spitzberg, B. 1981. Loneliness and communication apprehension. Paper presented at the Western Speech Communication Association convention, San Jose, CA.

Statistical Package for the Social Sciences, Inc. 1988. SPSS-X user's guide. 3rd ed. New York: McGraw-Hill.

Tinto, V. 1975. Dropout from higher education: A theoretical synthesis of recent research. *Review of Educational Research* 45:89–125.

Weiss, R. S. 1973. *Loneliness: The Experience of Emotional and Social Isolation*. Cambridge, MA: MIT Press.

Zakahi, W. R., and R. L. Duran. 1982. All the lonely people: The relationship among loneliness, communicative competence, and communication anxiety. *Communication Quarterly* 30:203–209.

5 Learning Through Letters: A Research Direction from the Margins

Susan May

Introduction

My research interest in letter writing has emerged from my experience of corresponding with distance students. I have been intrigued to discover that students' learning experiences are enhanced through letter correspondence with faculty, and even with other students. Like other forms of education, distance education is most effective when learners are central to the enterprise instead of marginal to it (The Group of Collaborative Inquiry 1993). Using a document analysis process, I have uncovered information which indicates that through letters distance students lose their marginality.

Since 1992 I have received many letters from distance students in my role as their faculty advisor. I consider it a privilege to correspond with these students because their letters have been remarkable; they are thoughtful, interesting, engaging and self-reflective. I have appreciated students' insights and their level of engagement in learning processes. As a result I have conducted research of a preliminary nature in order to better understand how letter writing improves the learning experiences of distance students. I believe this research is particularly important in the 1990s, when computer technology and the Internet threaten to change profoundly the nature of distance learning and teaching. I engaged in this research as an educator who values learning as a process, not solely as a product. I note in this regard Menzies' (1994) observation that the information highway has a bias "toward information production and consumption, not dialogue" (p. 2). In this paper I explain the context of the study and the process I used, then I develop the themes of how letters serve as text for enhancing learning.

The Context and the Process

At the Canadian university where I work, The Master of Adult Education program is delivered via distance education. The program has a professional development focus and a self-directed learning orientation. Students, in consultation with faculty, design individualized learning plans within a three phase program structure. There are academic requirements for literature reviews, project work, and theses. The students submit written reports to document their learning within each phase. Students have a five year candidacy period and participation in a three week orientation workshop is the only residential requirement. During orientation students are assigned to a faculty advisor who then works with them throughout their course of study.

Although there is no formal requirement for students to communicate with faculty advisors by letter, many do so. Other common forms of communication include telephone calls, e-mail messages, and sometimes in-person visits (depending on the student's geographic proximity to the campus). Because there is no requirement for letter writing, the letters I receive from students vary greatly in terms of style, purpose, length, and degree of formality. Typically, however, students communicate from personal perspectives about their families and jobs. The majority of letters also contain student observations, insights, and inquiries related to their personal and professional learning.

The students I supervise range in age from twenty to sixty-eight, and they reside in all ten Canadian provinces, as well as in several foreign countries. Students have diverse backgrounds with respect to their work specializations within the adult education field; their experience ranges, for example, from health education, to community college instruction, to private consulting, to human resource development.

Doing Research from the Margins. I believe that the most appropriate approach for researching the learning experiences of distance students is through the words of the students themselves. The subtitle of my paper, a research direction from the margins, therefore is designed not only to portray information about the margin notes of distance letter writers, but also to acknowledge that distance learners are often "on the margins of the production of knowledge" (Kirby and McKenna 1989, 17). By describing, quoting directly from, and analyzing the letters produced by distance learners, I intended to provide an honest portrayal of their experiences and opinions. The focus of the analysis is on student learning processes.

As a researcher I recognize that I, too, am subject to the enquiry, and that my experiences as a distance learner and educator influence the analysis. Like Kirby and McKenna (1989) I recognize that "theoretical examination must be strongly rooted in the very experience it claims to explain" (p. 20). My role as faculty advisor and correspondent with students is a factor in the study and has an impact upon student letter writing processes. Within the context of this study however, I focus exclusively on student letters; faculty letters and interchanges between them is the subject of a future investigation.

In this research initiative I have compiled evidence that supports my personal observations that letter writing can enhance the learning experiences of distance students. I use the Adult Education program in which I work as a case study. As a result my findings are descriptive in nature and preliminary. Archer (1994) supports the usefulness of such an approach by suggesting "there is evidence indicating that descriptive studies are exactly what is needed for the professional development of expert distance and adult educators" (p. 7).

Document Analysis. In the initial phase of this research (between February, 1994 and March, 1995) I reviewed the student files of the sixty-five students whom I currently supervise. Letters were on file from fifty-eight students, and the number of student letters contained in the files ranged from one to twelve. Of the seven students who had never written to me, two lived in the local community and chose to have personal meetings with me, two were "non-starts," and three were students who had been in the program for less than six months and had not yet initiated contact with me. I counted only letters that were of a nonadministrative nature (i.e., not related to fee payment or university regulations).

In reviewing the letters I noticed great variation. Some letters were very brief and of only a paragraph or two in length. Their major function was that of introducing and accompanying academic work being submitted for grading purposes. Although I recorded and sorted these letters into data files, I did not include them in the study because I focused my analysis upon student learning processes, rather than on products of learning. I also did not include postcards or short e-mail messages in my data analysis.

Remaining was a collection of 109 letters, which were of greater length and frequently of an "update" nature. In them students advised me of how their program work was progressing. They also described changes that were occurring within their worksites and careers as well as activities they were engaged in with their families and a variety of community organizations.

I created data files for all of the letters, and then coded passages and paragraphs in the letters according to the type of messages being communicated. I reviewed the data frequently and eventually grouped coded material together into larger categories that emerged as I reflected upon the material. I did so by moving data between categories until coherence became evident and key themes emerged. In presenting my findings I integrate data presentation and analysis and draw upon letters written by other students to other faculty within the program, as appropriate.

Letters as Text

These student letters provide the text from which I have analyzed their learning processes. Through their letter writing students have provided documentary evidence about how they frame their learning and how they understand their personal and professional development. I have categorized the most prevalent learning processes under three themes: developing visibility and voice, writing autobiographically and collaboratively, and constructing and contextualizing knowledge.

Developing Visibility and Voice. Because distance learners are largely invisible on college and university campuses, their needs are often neglected. A letter from Jane provides an example of this, within the context of lobbying a large university to offer distance courses in her isolated community.

> Last week someone in the registrar's office at the U of T asked me if I couldn't commute for intercessional courses which run week-day evenings from six to nine. I suggested that she find Moosonee on a map and explained that I not only couldn't drive the ten hours to Toronto and ten hours back on a daily basis, but that since there are no roads in and out of Moosonee I would have to pay $300 a day to fly to the nearest town with a road. This seemed to blow her mind, but at least she didn't make any other helpful suggestions!

This passage from Jane's letter alerts me to her frustrations. It is an understatement to suggest that educational institutions have failed in the past to recognize and understand her circumstances as a distance student. Given the clarity of her writing, however, I note that although Jane may lack physical visibility, she effectively makes her presence known.

Letters also provide a vehicle for students to express themselves and to assess their unique experiences and viewpoints. For example, Jill told me in a letter about her struggle to understand the relationship between personal and professional learning. She wrote:

> I see the area of reflection in adult learning as an extremely important and largely underrated aspect of many forms of learning....This reflective approach fosters an integration between professional learning and personal learning. As a therapist who has worked in two sole charge positions and in private practice I believe that the primary mode of professional development for me has been through reflection on my own practice and through networking.

In reflecting upon the uniqueness of her learning process, she communicates through letters how she "found the idea of individual constructs of the meaning of experience to be a particular breakthrough." She also relates how satisfied she is with, and encouraged by, the learning process she is engaged in.

Letter writing as a forum for student conversation appears to develop, in part, from students' increased visibility as they communicate with faculty personally and authentically. For example, in response to a letter I wrote to Anne, she says, "Thank you for your assistance. I think what I needed to do was write from my experience rather than trying to produce a technical paper which did not say anything about what was happening in my world." The text of Anne's letters suggests that she felt supported and encouraged to write about her personal learning and unique experiences. Letters provide an outlet through which students have opportunities to become subjects of their learning and protagonists of their stories (May 1995).

Some of the evidence I have documented suggests that students develop voice through "talking on paper." Letter writing appears to encourage students like Wendy to value their own learning and experience:

> Speaking about feeling that no one cares about what I'm doing I just wanted to mention how much I appreciate the time you put into commenting on my journal entries. Your response came at a grey time of year around here, and I was really energized by the fact that someone else seemed to think my work and reflection on it was worthwhile.

Letter writing, in this case, appears to provide Wendy with an opportunity to reflect upon her work. As a result her writing is not confined to the production of assignments nor content mastery exclusively. Instead, writing takes the form of thoughtful and professional conversations (McAlpine 1992).

The texts of student letters also describe how students like Gail develop thinking skills through writing. She writes: "Thanks for your patience in working your way through my 'thinking on paper.' Your comment about 'writing is a work in progress' has been a turning point for me—I keep a sign up above my desk as a reminder. It helps to process my thoughts in this way." To dialogue in this way also suggests to students that their learning is not confined to a rigid and autocratic curriculum.

Writing Autobiographically and Collaboratively. Much of the context of student letters relate to autobiographical writing and collaborative learning. Students not only write from their personal perspectives and social locations, but they also struggle with communicating their learning to a particular audience. June, for example, writes,

> I have struggled with the question of writing autobiographically. I have, like most women, experienced many forms of abuse—educational, institutional, having to witness the objectification of

women, loss of power in relationships and an abuse of power in work situations. However, I do not situate myself as a survivor within my academic work, but as a woman who has chosen to work with abused women.

I observe that students like June first communicate their own story before broadening their analysis to a larger social context. Critical analysis is a key process in this learning, as is recognition that subjectivity is a foundation for understanding knowledge and theory. Similarly, Janet writes:

> My reading schedule has slowed down since I started reading books on women and society, learning, working etc. It became very personal for me and I couldn't stay objective and removed from the content. For my own personal growth and development, I am going to have to go through the process of redefining my experiences, relationships, goals and whatever else becomes unsettled as I explore new information.

As documented by Merriam and Clark (1993) learning takes on increased significance for learners when they critique their experience as important and value this experience within their particular meaning system. Letter writing as a communication vehicle, provides a context for doing so. I note, in this regard, that Sandra wrote, "writing to you is like articulating to myself this 'brainwork' that I have been doing."

Another theme that emerges in student letters relates to audience. Students speak about this in terms of both their constituting an audience for other writers, as well as directing their writing to a particular audience. Terry, for example, writes:

> I am learning about "audience" from the various scholarly works that I have been reading. Those works that have particular impact for me are those which reach out to engage not only my mind but my spirit and my emotions. The dispassionate voice of the scholarly style is far less powerful than the personable voice because I am far more likely to learn from work that is written in a dialogic style.

The topic of audience appears to be a particularly interesting one in the field of distance education, where audiences frequently are invisible and relatively silent. Student letters suggest that faculty advisors as recipients of letters serve as a key audience for student learning.

Constructing and Contextualizing Knowledge. Frequently in letters students demonstrate interest in learning to transfer and apply knowledge from one context to another. For example, Donna communicates her struggle with articulating her native ways of knowing within a Western academic context.

> I am a prime example of the learners that I write about in the training manual (I developed). I was neither raised, nor taught the cultural philosophy and practices of my own people until I returned to the reservation in 1984 to purposely seek this knowledge. I have spent 10 years trying to reclaim and to understand my own heritage, culture and language. My assimilation into Western culture, like the aboriginal learners I write about, was incomplete....I have benefited from a process which required me to be able to document and articulate the educational practices of my own people.

In this way, students use letters as a means for identifying problems, analyzing relevant factors, and developing strategies and action approaches.

I observe that letters provide a specialized learning context in which specific environmental and governmental issues impacting upon students' lives are analyzed and discussed. I note with interest that students write letters about world events like the Gulf War and the South African elections, and integrate learning from these events into their work. In this way students' learning frequently extends beyond the dominance of Western viewpoints and broadens to include global and underrepresented perspectives (Hall 1994).

Students who have worked in Third World contexts, frequently write letters about their work in applying theory appropriately to practice. Ellen describes such a process:

> I am working with a group of semi-literate women orienting them to start a micro-enterprise. I'm using popular education techniques that I have learnt about from reading and participating in popular theater workshops and it is all coming together.

Ellen further discusses how she applied principles related to needs assessment, safety, praxis, and accountability (Vella 1994) to her work. She also wrote about women's oppression within an economic and political context in Guatemala.

> The theme of my thesis is the development of economic literacy for womyn (sic). I believe that unless we understand economic concepts we can never participate fully in the economy. Instead, we will be controlled by the economy and the economic crisis is desperate here. I feel very strongly that economic justice is a space to work in.

In this way, students like Ellen assume critical approaches to knowledge production and to adult education practice. Students use letter writing as a way of processing and contextualizing some of this learning. In the process they gain insights about how adult education knowledge and practice is grounded in economic, historical, political, and social contexts (Sheared 1994).

Conclusions

In this research paper I have documented that student learning can be enhanced through letter writing and that some barriers associated with distance education are neutralized as a result. I acknowledge, however, that my findings are preliminary and nongeneralizable. Preliminary findings suggest that distance students assume active roles in creating and applying knowledge through letter writing, and that they become visible, active, and articulate learners.

Letter writing appears to offer students a practical, participatory approach to distance learning. In the process of examining their experiences, students develop skills of self-direction and reflection. Collaboration with faculty advisors is considered to be an essential feature of this teaching and learning approach, as attested to by Joanne:

> I hope you have not abandoned your plans to write a paper on letter-writing as a powerful learning opportunity. As I hope I have written to you in all my correspondence, your letters to me are invaluable. Your warmth, humor, specific comments and suggestions spur me on (although you would never know it by the lack of concrete evidence). Without your continued written encouragement, there is no doubt in my mind that I would have abandoned the program long ago.

Letter writing can facilitate relationship building between students and faculty advisors. Communicating with faculty via letters also appears to provide opportunities for students to negotiate understandings of their particular institutional cultures, both at work and school (Grace 1994).

Collins (1993) advocates that "methodology and standardized materials should not be allowed to define educational contexts" (p. 112). I concur with his claim and am concerned that distance education frequently takes a programmed and homogenized approach to instruction. I am grateful to my distance students, therefore, for demonstrating the benefits of letter writing. I do not claim that it is the only effective distance learning approach, nor that it is effective for everyone. I do suggest, however, that it offers opportunities from which students can benefit and, therefore, should be incorporated into existing delivery systems as appropriate.

Research Directions

Further research is needed with larger and more diverse populations of students and with distance educators who use letter writing in a variety of distance education contexts. I am particularly interested in investigating effective approaches and techniques for encouraging letter writing—ways that promote active and critical thinking and knowledge production. I speculate that critical reflection is key to the learning advantages experienced by students who employ letter writing, so I am also interested in investigating whether electronic forms of letter writing can be utilized effectively, as well. However, I also question whether some student populations are resistant to letter writing as a teaching tool and learning strategy. In future investigations I propose to expand my research methodology beyond document analysis and to involve co-investigators (including students) in both data collection and analysis. My ultimate goal is to have distance educators employ my research findings in ways that enhance and improve the learning experiences of distance students.

References

Archer, W. 1994. Theory and practice in the training of adult and distance educators. In *Proceedings of the 13th Annual Canadian Association for the Study of Adult Education Conference,* 7–10. Vancouver, BC.

Collins, M. 1993. New prospects for program planning and evaluation in adult continuing education. In *Proceedings of the 12th Annual Canadian Association for the Study of Adult Education Conference,* 108–113. Ottawa, ON.

Grace, M. 1994. Meanings and motivations: Women's experiences of studying at a distance. *Open Learning* 9(1):13–21.

Hall, B. 1994. Re-centring adult education research: Whose world is first? In *Proceedings of the 13th Annual Canadian Association for the Study of Adult Education Conference,* 190–195. Vancouver, BC.

Kirby, S., and K. McKenna. 1989. *Experience, Research, Social Change: Methods from the Margins.* Toronto, ON: Garamond Press.

May, S. 1995. Rediscovering an old technology: Personalizing learning through letters. *Adult Learning* 6(4):17–19.

McAlpine, L. 1992. Learning to reflect: Using journals as professional conversations. *Adult Learning* 3(3):15–24.

Merriam, S., and C. Clark. 1993. Learning from life experience: What makes it significant? *International Journal of Lifelong Education* 12(2):129–138.

Menzies, H. 1994. Learning communities and the information highway. *Journal of Distance Education* 9(1):1–16.

Sheared, V. 1994. Giving voice: An inclusive model of instruction—a womanist perspective. *New Directions of Adult and Continuing Education* 61:27–37.

The Group for Collaborative Inquiry. 1993. The democratization of knowledge. *Adult Education Quarterly* 44(1):43–51.

Vella, J. 1994. *Learning to Listen: Learning to Teach.* San Francisco: Jossey Bass.

6 Interactivity in Distance Education Television: A Constructed Reality

Catherine P. Fulford and
Shuqiang Zhang

Interactivity: A Constructed Reality

Interactivity in a two-way television setting is both a technological concept and a psychologically constructed reality. Kozma (1991) developed two theoretical constructs that agree with this notion. As a technological concept, the medium is only a channel through which information passes to and from the learner. The psychological concept, in contrast, is the interaction or relationship between the learner and the instructor represented through the medium. Since real-time interaction through current technological means can closely approximate face-to-face communication, it would seem that the medium would create the same results as a regular classroom. However, when Miller, McKenna, and Ramsey (1993) compared students' attitudes and achievement at studio and remote sites, there were significant differences in the students' feelings of mastery of the content and attitude toward interaction. Interestingly, when the on-campus group became a "remote" site, the differences also occurred. Does this mean that the psychological perception of the learner may overshadow the technical ability to create an approximation of a real classroom?

Attributes of the technological means alone are inadequate to account for instructional effectiveness. The effectiveness of the technology is mediated by human perceptions of the technology. Wagner (1994), in constructing a functional definition of interaction, warns that "fascination with what the technologies do often supersedes the broader issue of teaching and learning dynamics" (p. 7). An instructional interaction is "an event that takes place between a learner and the learner's environment. Its purpose is to respond to the learner in a way intended to change his or her behavior toward the goal" (p. 8). Salomon's (1983, 1984) model proposes that the amount of learning via a given medium is proportional to the amount of invested mental effort (AIME). Students tend to live up to their own psychological preconceptions of what their class should be like and this may color their perceptions. In Salomon's study, students perceived their television medium to be less difficult than print.

Miller, McKenna, and Ramsey (1993) advise that the perception that "television is easier" may not occur when the system provides two-way interaction; the real time, conversational capability can simulate a regular classroom. When examining interaction, researchers should consider the rudiments of the communication process—normal conversation. Cognitive speed theory demonstrates that the mind can comprehend information delivered at twice the speed of normal speech to allow for preparing responses (Fulford 1993). If our average rate of speech is comfortable when we are involved in a two-way conversation, what happens when we perceive ourselves as inactive in one-way communications like lectures and video programs? Kozma (1991) cautions, that a "virtual medium" is created by the attributes used during a session. Some instructors may be adept at using the technology to create a dynamic visual and verbal exchange. Other instructors uncomfortable with the setting may use a talking head approach. The medium becomes a static, one-way delivery system. Jonassen (1985) stipulates that the appearance of two-way communication must take place for interaction to occur. The learner's constructed reality of interaction is dependent on human interchange rather than just the capabilities of the technology.

How Is the Reality of Interaction Constructed? A Three-Year Research Agenda

The purpose of this paper is to describe studies on interaction in the Hawaiian Interactive Television System (HITS). A three-year research agenda has focused on three aspects of the reality of interaction constructed by students: a) the relationship between interaction time and the perception of interactivity, b) the relationship between satisfaction and the perception of interactivity, and c) perceived barriers to interactivity. The research is currently being expanded in two additional areas: changes in perceptions of barriers to interaction due to increased exposure to interactive television (ITV) and interaction strategies used across disciplines. Another related study has examined the differences in attitudes of students in one-way video sites versus two-way video sites.

The Setting. HITS, a 4-channel interactive inter-island closed-circuit television network, serves the University of Hawaii and other state and county agencies. HITS uses both Instructional Television Fixed Service (ITFS) and point-to-point microwave signals to connect six classrooms across the state. There are three origination sites on the main campus of Oahu and one each on the islands of Hawaii and Maui. The student population is predominantly Asian.

The origination sites have a full set of television monitor screens monitoring all the sites. The instructor is allowed to determine the classroom arrangement. The site monitors are placed at the back of the classroom, the program monitors in the front. In some cases the monitors serve as the bottom of a U-shaped design allowing the students to see students at other sites. Typically, instructors choose more traditional face-forward or U-shaped designs. Students must turn around completely or partially to see other sites on the monitors.

The students communicate directly with the other sites using individual or shared microphones on each desk. Receive sites have one or two program monitors, but no site monitors. The students only see information controlled by the instructor or technician. Other students typically appear on the screen only when they speak. Except for the audio-only sites, cameras in the front of the classroom record student activity. Indirect communications using e-mail and fax are encouraged, but all sites do not have equal access to the technology.

The Relationship between Interaction Time and the Perception of Interactivity. With regard to interaction time and perception of interactivity, the following research questions were investigated: Does the level of interaction perceived by students correspond to the actual amount of time spent on interaction in distance learning? Does an increase in interaction time result in a student attitude more favorable toward interaction in a distance learning environment? Is student perception of the level of interaction in the TV classroom determined mainly by personal participation or observation of participatory behaviors of other members of the class? (Zhang and Fulford 1994).

To conduct research, a video evaluation instrument was designed to measure the amount of interaction actually occurring in the two-way television classroom (Fulford and Zhang 1994). A survey instrument was developed to measure student perceptions of interaction in a 10-session interactive TV course with an enrollment of 260 students. Given the importance of interaction, one would expect students to respond positively when the amount of interaction time increased. Surprisingly when the relationship between student perceptions of classroom interaction and the actual amount of time allocated for interaction were examined (Zhang and Fulford 1994), no significant relationship was found between actual interaction time and student perception of interaction level; nor was student attitude towards interaction significantly related to interaction time. Student attitudes toward interaction were highly correlated with overall level of interactivity as perceived by students.

The Relationship between Satisfaction and Perception of Interactivity. The research questions for the study of satisfaction and perception of interactivity were: What is the relationship between learners' perceived personal level of interaction and their perceived level of overall interaction? How well does the perceived level of personal interaction predict one's satisfaction toward instruction? How well does the perceived level of overall interaction predict one's satisfaction toward instruction? Is there a relationship between the learners' perceived levels of both types of interaction combined and the satisfaction they feel toward the instruction? Do perceptions of interaction change over time?

Students' assessment of overall interactivity was found to be largely based upon vicarious participation rather than overt personal involvement (Fulford and Zhang 1993). Significant correlations were found between perceptions of personal and overall interaction. Perceptions of personal interaction were a moderate predictor of satisfaction. The critical predictor of satisfaction was the perception of overall interaction. This suggests that when learners perceive interaction to be high, they will have more positive satisfaction toward instruction than when interaction is perceived as low. Overall dynamics in interaction may have a stronger impact on learners' satisfaction than strictly personal participation. Vicarious interaction with the whole class may result in greater learner satisfaction than divided attention to overt engagement of each participant. However, perceived level of interaction and satisfaction seem to decline with increased exposure to interactive TV instruction.

Perceptions of Barriers to Asking and Answering Questions. Since learner perceptions are so important to their constructed reality of interaction, the next step in the research was to examine the barriers students perceived in interacting. The study examined the rudimentary elements of asking and answering questions (Sholdt, Zhang, and Fulford 1995). There were three research questions regarding barriers of asking and answering questions: Do learners at the studio site and remote sites perceive it easier to ask and answer questions in the traditional class or the interactive TV class? When interacting with the instructor, does the learner's location (studio or remote) affect the perceived ease of asking and answering questions? When interacting with other learners does the sender's location (studio or remote) and the receiver's location, the destination (same or different), affect the perceived ease of asking and answering questions?

Using a Likert scale survey, learner perceptions were collected from 235 individuals from both studio and remote sites in eleven HITS courses. Surprisingly learners from the remote site locations rated the interactive TV classroom as significantly easier for asking and answering questions than the traditional setting, while learners from the studio groups did not rate the two situations as significantly different. The learner location (studio or remote) or type of communication (ask or answer) did not have a significant effect on learner perceptions of the ease of communicating with the instructor. When asking and answering questions with other learners, learners at the remote site perceived these communication behaviors as significantly easier than learners at the studio sites. Overall, learners perceived sending answers to be easier than asking questions when communicating with learners at a different site, but they found asking questions to be easier than answering questions when communicating with learners at the same site. These results indicate that the learner constructed reality of interaction is far more complex than previous research has revealed.

Interactive Television with Two-Way and One-Way Video. To further examine learner perceptions, Zhang and Fulford (1995) investigated the effects of partial absence of video monitoring on student attitudes in an interactive television course. A comparison was made between learners located at sites with and without video feedback to the instructors. Data were collected for four variables: level of interaction as perceived by the students, value of the content taught, student assessment of gains in knowledge, and overall satisfaction. MANOVA results indicated that student perceptions of interaction were not affected by the absence or presence of video monitoring. The effect size was estimated to be practically zero. Does this mean that the video feedback to the instructor is totally irrelevant? Probably not, the instructors in this study were able to see more than 50% of the students on all occasions. Although not all students could be seen by the teacher, all students could see the instructor equally as well. This might help allay concerns that one-way video site students are at a disadvantage.

Changes in Perceptions of Barriers to Interaction Due to Increased Exposure to ITV. Another study has been designed to examine student perceptions of barriers to interaction in the interactive TV classroom. Data has been collected from 235 students across eight disciplines in eleven courses. A questionnaire was given to students at the beginning and end of the semester. The research questions were: What pre-conceived perceptions of barriers, if any, are brought into the TV classroom? What type of in-class interaction, if any, is perceived as unsuitable for TV instruction? How does an increasing amount of exposure to interactive TV influence such pre-conceived perceptions? What differences in such perceptions, if any, exist among the various disciplines that use the HITS system?

Interaction Strategies Used across Disciplines. What kinds of strategies are instructors using to create interaction in the classroom and are they effective? One study is currently being conducted to examine interaction strategies used across disciplines. Techniques and methodologies can vary greatly and there rarely is an opportunity to discover what is working for someone else. The goal of this descriptive research is to create a compilation of methods used across disciplines for increasing interaction in the television classroom. Video tapes of nine classes are being analyzed to determine what strategies are used, how often they are used, and how successful the strategies are. The Apple Newton® is being used to collect and compile observable data in five categories: personalization strategies, questioning strategies, motivation strategies, student-to-student strategies, and delayed interaction strategies.

Implications for Two-Way Interactive Television

System Design. The system characteristics of two-way television seem to create greater barriers between learners across sites than between learners and the instructor or learners at their own site (Sholdt, Zhang, and Fulford 1995). The lack of ability for the teacher to see every site does not seem to change perceptions of the level of interactivity (Zhang and Fulford 1995), but it may affect students' ability to interact with other students (Sholdt, Zhang, and Fulford 1995). Commonly there is no visual contact between learners at the various sites until the instructor or technician chooses to show an individual, group of students, or site on the program monitor. TV monitors for all sites are often only present at the studio site, and depending on the set-up may not be easily visible even by the studio learners. In an interview with students at a remote site, students said that it was easier to interact with the instructor than with the other sites simply because you can see them. Whenever students from other sites were put on the screen, interaction became easier. In a traditional teacher-centered approach, lack of student-to-student interaction may seem relatively unimportant. However, to improve results with student-centered learning, future research should examine ways to reduce visual barriers that inhibit student-to-student contact, particularly contact across sites.

Instructional Design. Instructional design may be able to provide more cost effective solutions than system alterations. Researchers should consider evaluating strategies that increase student-to-student interaction. Strategies to increase the visibility of individual students and learner-to-learner activities across sites may increase the students' connection to each other and improve learner centered instruction. Electronic mail and other personal communications could serve as a vital link for collaborative projects. Students should be encouraged to share their thoughts with others in the system rather than depending only on their site mates for interaction. Could strategies that increase learner-to-learner involvement have an affect on the learner constructed reality of interaction?

Although previous studies have suggested increasing interaction (Garrison 1990; Ritchie and Newby 1989; Yarkin-Levin 1983), more recent studies (Fulford and Zhang 1993; Zhang and Fulford 1994) show that increasing the level of interaction is not enough. Specific strategies have to be designed to change learner perceptions. Since perceived level of interaction is highly correlated with attitude toward interaction and satisfaction, teachers need be made aware that class atmosphere can be improved only on students' terms. Teacher designed interactive activities perceived as irrelevant will not improve attitude or motivation, regardless of how much time is reserved for such activities. Developing a sensitivity to the students' perspective is more important than subscribing to an abstract theory of cooperative learning or a conveniently packaged repertoire of activities.

In the past, interaction has been treated as a generic teaching technique. Instead, maybe it should be treated as a learning outcome. Since perception and satisfaction are affective characteristics, learners should be made aware that their perceptions of interaction are linked to their satisfaction. They must understand that their own level of participation is important so that the overall participation of the class is increased. Teachers may want to involve learners in designing strategies to improve participation and make them responsible for their own learning and interaction. Researchers should examine how interaction designed as a learning outcome may change learners' perceptions of interaction.

Overall dynamics in interaction seem to have a stronger impact on learners' satisfaction than strictly personal participation (Fulford and Zhang 1993). Vicarious interaction may result in greater learner satisfaction than individual interaction. Instructors teaching through interactive TV probably should be more concerned with the overall dynamics rather than equally distributed attention to engaging every individual or soliciting overt individual responses. More research is needed to further define the concept of vicarious interaction and determine its role in learner perceptions.

With the passage of time learner perception of interaction and satisfaction may decrease (Fulford and Zhang 1993). Perception of interaction becomes a more stable predictor of satisfaction as learners become more experienced with technology. Future studies are necessary to determine whether a shift in perception and satisfaction is related to the amount of repeated exposure to interactive TV. If so, new pedagogical strategies need to be developed to preclude the negative effect of long-term use of interactive TV. Opportunities should be provided that allow learners to continually use their new skill and be rewarded for interacting. Strategies would need be developed to encourage positive feelings about interacting in the distance education classroom.

Is interaction truly a constructed reality? If so, how can learner perceptions be influenced "by design"? The TV classroom poses new challenges to how education is viewed. Marked differences have been observed between the traditional classroom and the relaxed "TV room" ambiance sometimes occurring at distance sites. Research into the changing culture of the classroom created by distance education systems may be important to fully understand learners' perceptions of interactivity.

References

Fulford, C. P. 1993. Can learning be more efficient? Using compressed speech audio tapes to enhance systematically designed text. *Educational Technology* 33(2):51–59.

Fulford, C. P., and S. Zhang. 1993. Perceptions of interaction: The critical predictor in distance education. *The American Journal of Distance Education* 7(3):8–21.

Fulford, C. P., and S. Zhang 1994. Tooling up to go the distance -- A video analysis tool for interaction in distance education. In *Proceedings of the National Convention for the Association for Educational Communications and Technology,* eds. M. R. Simonson, N. J. Maushak, and K. L. Abu-Omar 215–228. Nashville, Tennessee.

Garrison, D. R. 1990. An analysis and evaluation of audio teleconferencing to facilitate education at a distance. *The American Journal of Distance Education* 4(3):13–24.

Jonassen, D. H. 1985. Interactive lesson designs: A taxonomy. *Educational Technology* 25(June):7–17.

Kozma, R. B. 1991. Learning with media. *Review of Educational Research* 61:179–211.

Miller, J. W., M. C. McKenna, and P. Ramsey. 1993. An evaluation of student content learning and affective perceptions of a two-way interactive video learning experience. *Educational Technology* 13(6):51–55.

Ritchie, H., and T. J. Newby. 1989. Classroom lecture/discussion vs. live televised instruction: A comparison of effects on student performance, attitudes, and interaction. *The American Journal of Distance Education* 3: 36–45.

Salomon, G. 1983. The differential investment of mental effort in learning from different sources. *Educational Psychologist* 18(1):42–50.

Salomon, G. 1984. Television is "easy" and print is "tough": The differential investment of mental effort in learning as a function of perceptions and attributions. *Journal of Educational Psychology* 76:647–658.

Sholdt, G. P., S. Zhang, and C. P. Fulford 1995. Sharing across disciplines—Interaction strategies in distance education. Proceedings of the National Convention for the Association for Educational Communications and Technology. Anaheim, CA.

Wagner, E. D. 1994. In support of a functional definition of interaction. *The American Journal of Distance Education* 8(2):6–29.

Yarkin-Levin, K. 1983. Anticipated interaction, attribution, and social interaction. *Social Psychology Quarterly* 46:302–311.

Zhang, S., and C. P. Fulford. 1994. Interaction time and psychological interactivity: Are they the same thing in the TV classroom? *Educational Technology* 34(4):58–64.

Zhang, S., and C. P. Fulford 1995. Interactive TV with two-way and one-way video. Unpublished manuscript, University of Hawaii at Manoa, Department of Educational Psychology and Department of Educational Technology, Honolulu, HI.

7   The Use of Computer Networks in Distance Education. Analysis of the Patterns of Electronic Interaction in a Multinational Course

Yolanda Gayol

The purpose of this research was to use transactional distance theory to explore the transactions that occurred in the computer mediated communication (CMC) environment of an integrated multimedia distance education course having an international group of students.

Theoretical Framework

The theory of transactional distance (Moore 1983) describes the universe of pedagogical relationships existing in an educational situation characterized by physical and spatial separation of the teacher and learners. According to this theory, the distance between the teacher and the learners is not just a physical phenomenon, but a pedagogical and psychological barrier to be overcome, either through face-to-face or through remote interaction. It is possible to overcome the distance through a careful balance between dialog and structure. This balance is the result of decisions made during program design and consists of

- the proportion of structured activities organized for a course,
- the proportion of time invested for the dialog on each session,
- the stimulation of an exchange of ideas, and

- the establishment of a friendly environment within a learner-centered relationship.

In Moore's theory, interaction is not just the technological availability of two way synchronous communication, but is a key variable to be manipulated in the instructional design. Thus it is important for designers to decide, carefully and consciously, the relative proportions of interaction between student and student, student and instructor, student and content needed to achieve the educational goals of a course. In this view, interaction is not designed for a uniform mass of students but may vary according to the needs and taking into account the learning styles of each individual learner.

Methodology

The course studied in this research was entitled Introduction to Distance Education and explored the content of distance education. Offered by The Pennsylvania State University, the course was delivered to seven sites located in three countries, the United States, Mexico, and Finland. The course utilized a combination of print-, audio- and video-based materials; a multimedia program; and audioconferencing, as well as computer mediated conferencing (CMC). Audioconferences were held on Saturdays, to allow for time differences between Europe and North America, and consisted of two sessions of three hours each for seven weeks. This particular course had a total of 200 hours of study with sixty-five student participants.

A two dimensional instrument to capture information posted by CMC was designed on the basis of the theory of transactional distance (Moore 1983). This instrument was pilot-tested by reading and analyzing the information posted by CMC during the first month. After a few adjustments, we proceeded to capture information through the remainder of the course. Analysis of the CMC postings included measurement of both the frequency and intensity of e-mail interactions. The extent and nature of these interactions are considered variables indicating the autonomy and self-direction of the student.

The concept of transactional distance includes the total environment of communication established between an instructor and the students. Dialog is a concept describing interaction of an exclusively positive nature, in which each participant is a respectful and active listener who contributes and builds on the contributions of others (Moore 1972, 1983, 1992). For this reason in this research we studied the learners' affective reactions through the e-mail messages as they showed how they valued interaction measured as a positive, neutral, or negative response to the instructional process they were experiencing.

The concept of structure, as described in the theory, was represented by the posting of required assignments. The ability to manage posted assignments was considered as evidence of a student's ability to deal with the content itself. This is very important because in computer mediated communication access to content is not immediate; there is the need to overcome previous barriers and relationships before the student can get to the core of the subject matter, These barriers are

- technological (the availability and dependability of the service),
- psychological (attitudes towards technology),
- educational (skills to navigate comfortably in the networks), and
- organizational (conditions and time to allow access to CMC). (Gayol 1995)

In this study a follow-up procedure was used to analyze all the public messages exchanged among the students, the instructors, and site coordinators posted through Decert-L, a listserv set up for this purpose. The variables measured were as follows:

- rates of participation in CMC throughout the course
- intensity of each individual's participation
- the timing of the first linkage to the listserv of each learner
- transactional distance, defined operationally for this medium in two dimensions with the assignments considered as the structure and dialog represented by the degree and nature of debate, i.e., the posting of additional information beyond the required posting of assignments and the positive or negative enunciations

More specifically, CMC postings were considered indicators of dialog if:

- the student posted e-mail messages in addition to the required assignments;
- the messages posted in the public list were directed at one student or sent to the virtual community;
- the academic communication was adding new information to enrich what was said previously on e-mail or audioconferencing;
- the exchange of messages promoted the debate or academic criticism;
- the communication was of a professional nature, that is, if e-mail messages were related to the jobs of the learners;
- the communication was of a cultural nature, i.e., the exchange of information concerned with the different cultural environments of this international virtual community; and
- the communication consisted of social conversation and to what extent this compared with the content-related communication.

In brief, the research looked at the proportion of activities that were highly structured (assignments) and those that were less structured (CMC interaction), the extent to which meaningful and thoughtful exchanges were induced, and the degree of learner-centered comfort that was established in the environment. Additionally, certain basic characteristics of the participants: age, gender, school level, and computer literacy were also determined.

Findings

Learner Characteristics

The characteristics of the learners in the course Introduction to Distance Education, taught during the Fall of 1993 were as follows. All students were adults with an average age of thirty-nine years. The U.S. participants were graduate students, taking the course for credit, and the learners at the international sites, enrolled on a non-credit basis, held bachelors' and graduate degrees, with the majority being undergraduate degree recipients. Most students were professionally involved in education-related activities. All of them were computer literate, but some were inexperienced in computer networking. The students at the international sites were trained in the use of electronic mail before the course started. It should be noted that the study did not include the learners at an additional site in Estonia, as they were in the process of setting up their networks and students started their participation late, and thus were not included in the study.

Table 1. Participants on CMC

Country	Site	Female	Male	Total
U.S.A.	University Park	13	4	17
U.S.A.	Monroeville	1	1	2
U.S.A.	Harrisburg	3	5	8
Mexico	UNAM	15	2	17
Mexico	UdeG	4	5	9
Finland	Turku	6	1	7
Finland	Lahti	1	4	5
Total		43	22	65

As shown above, 66% of the students were female and 34% male.

Participation

The participation among students, instructor, and site coordinators online was also tabulated as shown in Table 2.

Table 2. Percentage of Participation on CMC

Country	Site	September	October	November
U.S.A.	University Park	88% (15)	70% (14)	64% (11)
U.S.A.	Monroeville	50% (1)	50% (1)	50% (1)
U.S.A.	Harrisburg	50% (2)	25% (2)	12% (1)
Mexico	UNAM	77% (12)	17% (3)	5% (1)
Mexico	UdeG	44% (4)	33% (3)	11% (1)
Finland	Turku	71% (6)	71% (6)	28% (2)
Finland	Lahti	20% (1)	20% (1)	0% (0)
Overall participation		66%	43%	26%

Note: actual number of participants in parenthesis.

During the first month, 67% of the participants, that is, almost two-thirds of the students, were visibly accessing the e-mail listserv. This is important because it means they had overcome the barriers mentioned above, and they were able to establish electronic communication. It is more meaningful if we consider that the two Mexican sites had a new and still emerging infrastructure of telecommunications, and as was said before, some students had no previous experience accessing the Internet.

Frequency of Interaction

The University Park, Pennsylvania site had the highest rate of interaction (88%) and the overall highest rate of participation (63%). In addition, 66% of the students sent more than one message. Lahti, Finland, had the lowest rate of participation with only one of the five students with visible interaction and participation. The instructors of the course also sent some messages to the listserv so the relationship between instructor and learners was established in the first month.

During the following month the rate of participation declined from 67% to 43% of the students. If we consider with Wells (1992) that one-third of the learners are "lurkers" we could conjecture that about two-thirds of the participants, at most, had the benefits of CMC interaction during the second third of the course. During November, the rate of participation fell again from 47% to 26%. Just seventeen of sixty-five students were visible participants on Decert-L at the end of the course; by this point participation was almost solely among the U.S. students. It could be said there was a North Americanization of the communication channels.

The following qualitative variables were identified and explored through the analysis of the CMC postings.

Promotion of Debate

In the first third of the course, seventeen student initiated messages promoted the discussion of issues related to the course content. That is important because it reveals the student-content relationship, and it is an indicator of autonomy and self-directedness of the learners, in a new and faceless environment. University Park was the most active site in promoting the debate.

Adding Comments

This variable refers to the introduction of new ideas on the content being discussed, even though they are not critical nor promote debate. During the first third of the course, the forty-four online visible participants, sent twenty-five messages with new elements of discussion. This seems to be a good indicator of dialog among the students. When we compared this data with the interaction between sites, we noticed that just two of the seven sites, UNAM and University Park were interacting in this way. In future research this might be followed up, since this indicator, as well as the promotion of debate, could prove to be important qualitative indicators for evaluating the engagement and active participation of the learners.

We believe that adding comments to the ongoing discussion of content and promotion of debate were higher expressions of rational thinking, rather than simple description of topics. The researchers also recognize that CMC has an advantage over a face-to-face seminar because valuable ideas are not lost but kept and shared to be reflected on by the whole community of participants. Extending and deepening a debate in a multiple-media course encourages the development of the students' ability to engage in this type of expression. Other benefits of this kind of learning experience include the democratic spread of new thoughts and sharing of ideas.

Transactional Distance

During the first third of the course there were eighty-two positive statements related to the interaction provided through CMC. There were no negative expressions. Seven of the messages were neutral, meaning there were no qualifying adjectives. Neutral messages generally referred to the organization and administration of the course. Overall, the University Park site had the higher rate of positive expressions. The data on the dialog established among the learners is shown in Table 3.

Table 3. Dialog Among the Learners

	Debate			Adds Information			Approach Positive			Negative		
Months*	S	O	N	S	O	N	S	O	N	S	O	N
Country:												
USA	8	22	9	15	29	21	48	59	42	0	0	0
Mexico	2	1	3	4	1	6	27	9	12	0	0	0
Finland	0	5	0	0	6	0	7	9	3	0	0	0

*S= September, O= October, N= November

In September, almost two of three students sent more than one message (56.8%). This suggests that as a result of the structure of the course the dialog was initiated. Furthermore, thirty-one learners sent messages addressed to individuals; meaning that half of the individuals were answering posted questions and comments, yet another indicator that the dialogic relationship was established, albeit among and between less than half the class.

Also, in September the proportion of messages sent to the community of participants was two and one-half times higher than those sent to individuals. CMC was therefore fulfilling the goal of public communication. The social integration of the student group was working.

Professional and Cultural Information

The exchange of information on professional and cultural issues was unexpectedly low. We found that during the first month, there were just three messages concerning the field, the disciplines, or the professional activities of the participants. There were also few exchanges about cultural issues, even though the participants were from three different countries. The students' relationship therefore was highly task oriented.

Structure

Attention to and completion of required assignments were considered to be indicators of the effectiveness of the structure of the course and, in this case, we found that forty-four of the sixty-five reporting students posted the first assignment on CMC. This data could indicate that structure was functioning adequately. However, the posting of the assignments was a difficult indicator to measure because the study examined participation by individual students. In this course there was a great deal of team project work which did not always allow identification of the learners involved. Furthermore, the teams were unstable, since the same individuals did not always participate in the same teams.

In order to support the rapport among students, students were asked in the first assignment to relate their personal biographies, tastes, hobbies, and interests.

Table 4. Structured Activities (Assignments)

Rate of completion of assignments by assignment

Assignment	1	2	3	4	5	6	7
Country							
U.S.A.	70%	14%	29%	18%	29%	33%	44%
Mexico	50%	15%	30%	27%	8%	8%	0%
Finland	50%	0%	26%	0%	50%	100%	58%

Summary of Results

- Sixty-seven percent of the students made their first linkage within the first month.
- The rate of participation decreased as the course progressed.
- The "intensity" (frequency) of interaction increased for those students who continued to participate.
- U.S. students debated more and provided more additional information related to the content than international learners.
- The messages were highly task oriented; social, cultural, or professional issues did not appear spontaneously but just when they were requested by the instructor.
- The dialog became "Americanized."
- There was a high proportion of positive statements and few negative statements.

Regrettably, it was not possible to follow up the structured activities accurately; however, transactional distance theory was an invaluable tool to direct analysis of the interactions of this multinational group of learners.

Conclusions

From this exploratory research on computer mediated conferencing it appears that the main barriers to CMC communication had been overcome in the first month of the course. The levels of dialog were high in the same period and the promotion of debate and the additional comments posted added excitement to the learning process, as described by the learners at all of the sites.

Additionally, indicators of structure showed that the student-content relationship was promoted in this medium.

However, since there was a good interaction between learners, instructors, and moderators as well as highly positive attitude towards CMC communication, further investigation is needed to explain the decrease in the participation rates over the life of the course. In the case of UNAM site in Mexico, technological barriers affected the interaction rates. These included a change from IBM to VAX machine and a migration of users from bitnet to Internet at this particular site. This technological change immediately led to problems of connectivity among the learners. While they were allowed to use both systems during the transition, the need to acquire new technical knowledge was a "distraction from the communication of the course content." This problem added an extra workload for these particular students, which, added to the North-Americanization of the dialog and further discouraged participation at this site. However, the decrease also occurred at other sites, so there is a need to study national and international courses to determine if this problem is more universal and, if so, to explore the cause(s) of this phenomenon.

Americanization of dialog was a second phenomenon to be identified for further research, if we are interested in maintaining a balanced advantage of benefits gained through the use of this medium.

References

Gayol, Y. 1995. *El vso de redes de cómputo con fines de educación a distancia: Análisis de los patrones de interacción electronica en un grupo estudiantil multinacional*. México, Tesis Die 23.

Moore, M. G. 1972. Learner autonomy: The second dimension of independent learning. *Convergence* V(2) 76–8E.

Moore, M. G. 1983. On a theory of independent study. In *Independent Study,* ed. D. Seward, 16–31. London: Croom-Helm.

Moore, M. G. 1993. Theory of transactional distance. In *Theoretical Principles of Distance Education,* ed. D. Keegan, 22–39. London and New York: Routledge.

Moore, M. G., and C. N. Gunawardena. 1992. Bangkok Project: Theory and Philosophy of Distance Education. OnLine List Discussion: Lani@bootes.unm.edu, Oct. 12.

Wells, R. .1992. *Computer Mediated Communication for Distance Education: An International Review of Design, Teaching and Institutional Issues.* Research Monograph Number 6. University Park, PA: The Pennsylvania State University, The American Center for the Study of Distance Education.

8   The Conative Capacity of Receive Site and Studio Site Learners Enrolled in Satellite Delivered Instruction

Michaeleen A. Davis

Introduction

Why do some learners set and achieve more goals and higher goals than other learners? The answer to this question can be discovered by investigating the role of conation and the conative domain. Conation, which involves both motivation and volition, is described as the intent to act, striving, volitional control, or action control. The conative domain is associated with goal-directed action and goal accomplishment styles. Individuals who achieve goals may utilize better goal orientation strategies because they are intrinsically motivated and have more volitional control over their behavior. In other words, we can say those individuals have a higher conative capacity. How we set goals also depends on our psychological type. Jung (Atman 1990; Lawrence 1979) theorizes that psychological typology can be identified as two attitudes (introversion and extroversion) and four functions (thinking, feeling, sensation, and intuition). Distance learners are not unlike traditional classroom learners with respect to goal-setting styles and psychological types. The primary characteristic that distinguishes distance learners from traditional classroom learners is the separation by time or geographic location from the teacher. The distance teacher may not recognize the individuation of distance learners, therefore, it may be difficult for the distance teachers to adequately meet the needs of the distance learners (Atman 1987, 1990).

Statement of the Problem

A literature search of the conative capacity of distance learners produced a limited amount of related information. Further, a literature search revealed no research has been conducted in the area of the conative capacity and psychological typology of distance learners at receive sites and studio sites for satellite-based educational experiences. A close investigation of the interaction of conation, goal accomplishment style, and psychological type related to distance learners at receive sites and studio sites may provide distance educators (teachers, curriculum designers, and higher education institutions) with information to help in course design and delivery, and the design of instructional materials that recognize the individuation of and respond to the needs of distance learners at these sites.

This study investigated the interrelationship of conation, goal accomplishment style, and psychological type in learners at receive sites and learners at a studio site (on-campus) during transmission of a satellite delivered course. The specific research questions addressed in the study included:

1. What is the conative capacity of distance learners at receive sites and at the studio site as indicated through the Goal Orientation Index and supporting data?
2. What are the psychological types of distance learners at receive sites and at the studio site as indicated through the Myers-Briggs Type Indicator and supporting data?
3. Are there any differences between the elements of conation, goal accomplishment style, and psychological types in distance learners at receive sites and at the studio site?
4. What is the interrelationship of conation, goal accomplishment style and psychological type in distance learners at receive and studio sites?
5. What influence, if any, do distance teachers have on the conative capacity of distance learners at receive sites and at the studio site?

Theoretical Perspective

Shute (1992) focuses on conative aptitudes and describes them as "mental conditions or behaviors directed toward some event and include motivation, effort, volition, arousal, and striving" (p. 2). As described by Mezirow (1991), a learner exercises conation through a line of action or moving toward a goal. This description of conation includes desire, volition, and the intensity level of the learner to act. The cognitive, affective, and psychomotor domains are utilized by teachers and learners to specify and set goals (Johnson et al. 1991). In the conative domain (Atman 1987), an individual can consciously assess patterns of motivational behavior.

Conation, the intent to act, involves both motivation and volition (Corno 1993). Volition is the intervening process allowing the individual to stay focused on the task until completion (Deci and Ryan 1985; Park 1992). As a volitional construct, conation influences individuals to strive toward different goals because individual effort and personal experience has a different meaning for each person (Fritz 1991). Mastery-oriented learners are intrinsically motivated. They believe that ability improves as they learn new tasks, therefore, they exert more effort to set and achieve more realistic goals, and to increase and sustain the ability to learn new tasks. If they are motivated intrinsically, they will have a higher volitional level (Davis 1995; Park 1992).

How we envision our goals, stay motivated to achieve those goals, and increase our conative capacity depends on our individual psychological typology. Jung (Atman 1990; Lawrence 1979) theorizes that psychological typology can be identified as two attitudes: introversion and extroversion; and four functions: thinking, feeling, sensing, and intuition, and includes a conscious striving, willing, and desiring.

Saba (1990) indicates that goal-oriented teaching and purposeful learning are critical elements of distance education. Several dimensions must be present in distance education including: the learner, an objective of learning, course content, an end result, distance, and a medium to dispense the objective and/or course content. With the exception of distance, these dimensions are no different from those needed for learning to occur in the traditional classroom. Designers of and teachers in distance education must be aware of the conative characteristics (initiative, perseverance, determination) of the distance learner (Atman 1989).

Methodology

For the purpose of this study, receive site learners are defined as all students registered and enrolled in SATNET (6 S) graduate off-campus satellite delivered courses and Bridging the Gap (BG) undergraduate off-campus satellite delivered courses during the fall semester, 1994, at West Virginia University. Studio site learners are defined as graduate students registered and enrolled in a graduate on-campus satellite delivered course during the fall semester, 1994, at West Virginia University.

Data from the receive sites were collected from questionnaires, Goal Orientation Index (GOI), Myers-Briggs Type Index (MBTI), participant journals, and interviews. Data from the studio site were collected from questionnaires, Goal Orientation Index (GOI), Myers-Briggs Type Index (MBTI), participant journals, and follow-up questionnaires.

The initial questionnaires elicited demographic information about the participants and background information about the distance learners including their prior experience in distance education courses. The GOI provided information concerning an individual's "goal accomplishment style" by assessing the relative strengths and weaknesses in the goal accomplishment process. The MBTI provided information concerning the individual's personality or psychological type. The participants' journals reflected their habits and practices in setting individual, personalized goals; how they get and stay motivated; volitional practices when distracted, and reflective thoughts about the satellite delivered courses they are currently enrolled in.

The interview questions used with the receive site participants explored students' perceptions of goal-orientation activities, motivation, distractions in the learning environment, satellite course goals, satellite course assignments, distance teacher influences and practices. One participant from each MBTI category was selected to be interviewed. Follow-up questionnaires were used with the studio site participants to obtain similar information.

Analysis of Data

Questionnaires. Of the 301 questionnaires sent to receive site students, seventy-five were completed and returned for a return rate of approximately 25%. The data indicated that sixty-seven participants were female and eight were male. The majority of the participants were over age thirty-six, and 63% of the participants had prior experience in distance education courses. The participants responded that the technical problem encountered most often was audio phone bridge failure which resulted in not being able to communicate with the distance teacher. Of the twenty-three questionnaires sent to studio site students, twenty were completed and returned for a return rate of approximately 87%. The data indicated that nineteen participants were female and one was male. The majority of the participants were between age twenty-one and twenty-five. The data indicated that only one of the participants had prior experience in distance education courses. The participants responded that the technical problem encountered most often was poor audio quality from the receive sites.

Goal Orientation Index Scores. Of the seventy-five Goal Orientation Index instruments sent to receive site students, fifty-eight were completed and returned. The analysis of data from the Goal Orientation Index indicated that the top three areas of strength in the goal accomplishment process for receive site students were consistent with the data from Atman's 1985-1986 Norms Profile (N = 1116) in eight of the twelve categories on the GOI. The twelve categories are grouped into three phases (four categories per phase). Based on data received from the study, receive site students scored highest in the acting phase. They are not as strong in the planning phase, and they are least strong in the reflecting phase. These results were consistent with the data from Atman's 1985-1986 Norms Profile (N = 1116) which indicated that American adults scored highest in the acting category, not as strong in the planning category, and are least strong in the reflecting category.

Of the twenty-three Goal Orientation Index instruments sent to studio site students, nineteen were completed and returned. The analysis of data from the Goal Orientation Index indicated that the top three areas of strength in the goal accomplishment process for studio site students were consistent with the data from Atman's 1985-1986 Norms Profile (N = 1116) in nine of the twelve categories on the GOI. Based on data received from the study, studio site students scored highest in the acting phase. They are not as strong in the planning phase, and they are least strong in the reflecting phase. Once again these results indicate that American adults score highest in the acting category, not as strong in the planning category, and are least strong in the reflecting category.

Myers-Briggs Type Indicator Categories. Of the seventy-five Myers-Briggs Type Indicator instruments sent to receive site students, fifty-eight were completed and returned. Of the fifty-eight participants in the study, thirty are extravert and twenty-eight are introvert, thirty-seven prefer sensing and twenty-one prefer intuition, twenty-six make decisions based on thinking and thirty-two prefer to make decisions based on feeling, and forty-one prefer to live a life based on judging and seventeen prefer to live a life based on perceiving.

Of the twenty-three Goal Orientation Index instruments sent to studio site students, nineteen were completed and returned. Of the nineteen participants in the study, thirteen are extravert and six are introvert, sixteen prefer sensing and three prefer intuition, three make decisions based on thinking and sixteen prefer to make decisions based on feeling, and fifteen prefer to live a life based on judging and four prefer to live a life based on perceiving.

Paired Comparisons of the GOI and MBTI. For the statistical analysis of this study, paired t-tests were used to examine the relationship, closeness, or association between paired scores on the categories of the GOI and the types of the MBTI. Receive site participants who had a preference for the extraversion attitude and the intuitive function had a stronger goal accomplishment style profile on all twelve categories of the GOI, and goal accomplishment profiles of the participants who preferred the judging attitude was stronger in eight categories of the GOI. These results are consistent with the data from Atman's 1985-1986 Norms Profile (N = 1116). Participants who preferred to use the feeling function had a stronger goal accomplishment style in all twelve categories of the GOI. The feeling function appears to assist in the goal accomplishment process. These results are not consistent with the data from Atman's 1985-1986 Norms Profile (N = 1116) which indicated that American adults preferred the thinking function in ten of the GOI categories. Atman's 1985-1986 Norms Profile study included a generalized student population in regular, traditional classrooms, and the participants in this study may be exhibiting a commitment to both the content of the courses and the process of delivery, which is satellite delivered instruction.

Studio site participants who had a preference for the extraversion attitude exhibited a stronger goal accomplishment style in ten categories of the GOI, and participants who indicated a preference for the intuitive function had a stronger goal accomplishment style profile in seven categories of the GOI. These results are consistent with the data from Atman's 1985-1986 Norms Profile (N = 1116). Participants who preferred to use the feeling function had a significantly stronger goal accomplishment style in eight categories of the GOI. These results are not consistent with the data from Atman's 1985-1986 Norms Profile (N = 1116). Goal accomplishment profiles of the participants who preferred the judging attitude were stronger in one category of the GOI. There is not sufficient data in this preference to determine if the feeling function assists in the goal accomplishment process.

Journals. Of the seventy-five journals sent to receive site students, thirty-five were completed and returned. All participants were encouraged to record their thoughts for at least six weeks. The majority of the participants made a conscious effort to set and achieve realistic course goals including getting assignments completed ahead of schedule to avoid stress, and expressed the intrinsic motivation to get the letter grade of A instead of just a passing grade. The participants were motivated to achieve personal goals or complete class assignments because the instructors provided a wide variety of instructional methods and materials, provided positive feedback, and made the class more practical. Several participants were distracted by noise outside and inside the receive site during the broadcast. Technical problems such as no video, no audio, phone bridge failure, or a prolonged period of no transmission from origination site provided the opportunity to become so distracted that much effort was needed to refocus on the class when technical problems are corrected. Once the participants have been distracted, it is often difficult to refocus or get back "on track." Of those participants who were alone at the receive site, the majority expressed a feeling of loneliness and isolation because there was no one to discuss ideas with or work on group projects.

Of the twenty-three journals sent to studio site students, nineteen were completed and returned. Once again all participants were encouraged to record their thoughts for at least six weeks. The majority of the participants stated that attending the studio class reduced the in-class participation because of the problems and distractions of the off-campus sites. The participants also stated the televised course did not allow for interaction between teacher and studio class, the televised course was effective in teaching the material but lacked the intimacy between teacher and student, and the studio class found it difficult to communicate with the off-campus sites because they couldn't see their facial expressions or body language. The majority of the participants also stated that the environment of the studio (lights, cameras, and camera operators) was uncomfortable, and there was paranoia caused by the threat of being "caught on camera." Staying motivated was also a stated problem because the class was so impersonal, the technical problems were distracting, and the off-campus sites were monopolizing the class time. Several of the participants indicated that the teacher implied that the studio class had more benefits, but the participants did not see it that way. They indicated that the studio class had needs and commitments also, and that combining the two classes (studio and off-campus) is not a good idea. Each group needed the attention of the instructor who was giving more time and attention to the off-campus sites.

Interviews from Receive Sites. When queried about what they liked about the satellite course, the majority of the participants stated they enjoyed the convenience of having the course in their community and not having to drive two or three hours to campus for their course work. What the participants disliked the most was phone bridge failure and having difficulty making phone connection to the instructor in the studio. The participants expressed that the loss of immediate connection and face-to-face dialogue as in a traditional classroom is frustrating. Although the instructors did not influence the participants' behavior directly, there were numerous positive responses about the instructors' attitudes and teaching styles. The instructors provided positive feedback and reinforcement, employed a variety of teaching methods, and decreased the distance or the separation by making the class personal, practical, and stimulating. The participants indicated that although they were extrinsically motivated by achieving passing grades or getting assignments completed on time, they were intrinsically motivated to learn new techniques or ideas that would help them in their present or future jobs. The participants observed that teaching a satellite course is different than teaching a traditional course and that the instructors need distance education training before they teach through the satellite. The participants suggested that the instructors should adhere to the syllabus and not change or add additional workshops that require extra travel. In addition to not deviating from the syllabus, the participants suggest that when cooperative or group assignments are made, the instructors should remember that some groups members are separated from each other and communication must be made through mail, phone, or fax. The element of immediacy and intimacy is absent.

Follow-Up Questionnaires from Studio Site. When asked about what they liked about being in a studio site for a satellite delivered course, the majority of the participants stated they enjoyed the change from the regular classroom, and that they see that it is different if you are going to school part-time, working, and having a family. What the participants disliked the most was the long periods of time dealing with off-campus receive sites students and problems. The participants also expressed the lack of student/teacher relationship because the instructor made eye contact with the camera more than eye contact with the students in the studio. One of the participants stated that this class was not suitable for distance education because off-campus instruction is different than on-campus instruction. The instructor did not influence the participants' behavior directly and the studio class felt somewhat neglected. The participants indicated they were motivated by knowing that the semester was almost over and they would be happy with a grade. The participants were distracted by the lights and cameras in the studio and that it was difficult to move away from the distractions.

Discussion

Because distance learners are physically separated or isolated from the instructor, they must monitor their behavior and their progress in achieving personal and course goals. In essence, they must manage their learning throughout the course (Atman 1987) and be psychologically prepared to learn in isolation (Rumble 1981).

What is the conative capacity of distance learners at receive sites and at the studio site as indicated through the Goal Orientation Index and supporting data?

The results indicated no significant difference between the scores of the distance learners at receive sites and studio site and the general population of the 1985-1986 Norms group in all twelve categories of the GOI. Also, there was no significant difference in the scores of the distance learners at receive sites and at the studio site and the Norms group in the three phases of the GOI. The participants at the receive sites responded that although they were extrinsically motivated to work for a grade because their job depended on passing the course, a large majority of the participants indicated that they were intrinsically motivated to learn new skills and techniques that would help them perform their job more effectively. The studio site participants may not have been intrinsically motivated because they did not associate any practical application of the class to their present or future employment.

What are the psychological types of distance learners at receive sites and at the studio site as assessed through the Myers-Briggs Type Indicator and supporting data?

Data from the MBTI indicates that slightly more than half of the distance learners at the receive sites have a preference for extraversion, but when queried in the interviews whether they considered themselves extravert or introvert, several of the participants stated that when they were in class they had a different preference than when they were working or not in class. Data from the MBTI indicates that 68% of the studio site participants have a preference for extraversion, but when queried in the follow-up questionnaires whether they considered themselves extravert or introvert, they stated that it depended on the situation that they were in. Those participants who have a preference for extraversion are at a disadvantage because distance education, which favors the introvert, is a vicarious experience rather than direct, actual experience as in a traditional classroom. This can be the cause of much frustration, and compounding this frustration are the technical difficulties encountered when trying to communicate with the distance teacher through the phone bridge, and being in the studio when the distance teacher is interacting with the receive sites during phone bridge failure. Adding to the frustration of the extraverts at the studio site is the inability to have the teacher's attention when needed.

Are there any differences between the elements of conation, goal accomplishment style, and psychological types in distance learners at receive sites and at the studio site?

There was no significant difference between the extravert and introvert attitudes, the sensing and the intuitive functions, and the thinking and the feeling functions and goal accomplishment styles of the two groups on the categories of the GOI. There was, however, a significant difference between the judging and perception attitudes and goal accomplishment styles in eleven of the categories of the GOI, which appears related to the goal accomplishment process for distance learners at receive sites.

After reviewing the courses participants were enrolled in, it was determined that the majority of the participants are in areas or fields where the feeling attitude would be more prevalent. Distance learners who prefer the feeling function exhibit a stronger commitment to both the course content and to the process of delivery. Another fact that cannot be ignored is the high number of female participants in both groups which might explain the difference between the distance learners and the Norms group in the thinking and feeling function. Of the fifty-eight distance learners and nineteen studio site participants, seventy-one are females and the MBTI manual states that females had a tendency to respond with more feeling responses because certain feeling responses were more "socially desirable for females than males, or to the effect of social training" (Myers and McCaulley 1985).

What is the interrelationship of conation, goal accomplishment style, and psychological type in distance learners at receive and studio sites?

Examination of the journals, the interview data and the follow-up questionnaires revealed that individuals who have a high conative capacity are intrinsically motivated, are more effective in goal-setting techniques, and have more volitional control to overcome distractions, to stay focused, and to achieve their goals. Distance learners who can visualize the completed goals are more likely to achieve the goals. Learners at the studio site are not physically separated from the teacher, but they still must monitor their behavior and progress in achieving personal and course goals. Studio site learners must also have a high conative capacity, be intrinsically motivated, be more effective in goal-setting techniques, and have more volitional control to overcome distractions, to stay focused, and to achieve their goals. Based on the data collected in both studies, it can be concluded that the interrelationship of conation, goal accomplishment style, and psychological type in receive site learners and studio site learners is essential in designing and delivering effective distance education programs, and must be a collaborative effort between distance learners at receive sites, at the studio site, and distance teachers.

What influence do distance teachers have on the conative capacity of distance learners at receive sites and at the studio site?

The data indicated that the distance teachers did not have a direct influence on the conative capacity of the distance learners at the receive sites, nor did the instructor at the studio site, but for different reasons. Many of the distance teachers were excellent role models and mentors because they promoted learner self-confidence and self-efficacy, and made the courses personal by showing a genuine interest in their students. The studio site participants stated that the studio site distance teacher attended to the needs of the off-campus students more, and provided the off-campus students with more options for completing assignments than the studio site class. Further, the studio site participants indicated that the distance teacher was a novice distance teacher with no distance education training.

The interpretation of the questionnaires, journals, and structured interviews of the distance learners at the receive sites indicated that by understanding the personalities of the students, making the class personal and practical, and encouraging the setting and achieving of realistic and practical goals, the distance teacher can shorten the distance and reduce the feeling of isolation. This was not the case in the studio site class. In their journals and in conversation with the members of the studio class, they expressed the feeling of being distanced from not only the receive sites, but from the teacher as well. This may be the results of spending too much time on organizational type questions from the receive sites while the studio site participants sat in the studio.

Conclusions and Recommendations

Distance learners at receive sites as well as studio sites, must strive toward academic achievement through the conative domain, to stay intrinsically motivated, and to have a high volitional control over their behavior and learning. The continued use of the conative domain in distance education programs will continue to foster teaching effectiveness by helping distance and on-campus students become better learners and distance teachers become better facilitators. They must also continue to develop support or study groups within the receive sites, and to continue to build the collaborative effort with the distance teachers.

Distance teachers must know the conative capacity of the students and deem it necessary to incorporate the conative domain and conative objectives into the curriculum, or implement goal-setting activities into the courses. They need also to be aware of the individual difference and psychological types of *all* learners in order to provide facilitation through distance education resources. Distance teachers need to select the appropriate media type or adapt the method of delivery to meet the needs of *all* the learners.

References

Atman, K. S. 1987. The role of conation (striving) in distance education enterprise. *The American Journal of Distance Education* 1(1):14–24.

Atman, K. 1989. Goal accomplishment style and the long distance learner. Paper presented at the Annual Conference on Teaching at a Distance: Madison, Wisconsin.

Atman, K. 1990. Psychological type elements and goal accomplishment style: Implications for distance education. In *Contemporary Issues in American Distance Education*, ed. M. G. Moore, 136–150. Oxford: Pergamon Press.

Corno, L. 1993. The best-laid plans: Modern conceptions of volition and educational research. *Educational Researcher* 22(2):14–22.

Davis, M. A. 1995. The interrelationship of conation, goal accomplishment style, and psychological type in distance learners. Ed.D. diss., West Virginia University, Morgantown, West Virginia.

Deci, E. L., and R. M. Ryan. 1985. *Intrinsic Motivation and Self-determination in Human Behavior.* New York: Plenum Press.

Fritz, R. L. 1991. The association of selected conative variables to field-dependence with inferences for reasoning characteristics in marketing education. Paper presented at the Vocational Association Convention: Los Angeles, California.

Johnson, J. A., H. W. Collins, V. L. Dupuis, and J. H. Johansen. 1991. *Introduction to the Foundations of American Education,* 8th ed. Needham Heights, MA: Allyn and Bacon.

Lawrence, G. D. 1979. *People Types and Tiger Stripes.* Gainsville, FL: Center for Applications of Psychological Type, Inc.

Myers, I. B., and M. H. McCaulley. 1985. *Manual: A Guide to the Development and Use of the Myers-Briggs Type Indicator.* Palo Alto, CA: Consulting Psychologists Press, Inc.

Mezirow, J. 1991. *Transformative Dimensions of Adult Learning.* San Francisco, CA: Jossey-Bass.

Park, S. 1992. Motivational beliefs, volitional control, and self-regulating learning. Ph.D. diss., The University of Michigan, Ann Arbor, Michigan.

Rumble, G. 1981. Evaluating autonomous multi-media distance learning systems; A practical approach. *Distance Education* 2(1):64–90.

Saba, F. 1990. Integrated telecommunications systems and instructional transaction. In *Contemporary Issues in American Distance Education,* ed. M. G. Moore, 344–352. Oxford: Pergamon Press.

Shute, V. J. 1992. *Learning Processes and Learning Outcomes.* Brooks AFB, TX: Armstrong Lab. Human Resources Directorate.

9 The Application of Synergetic Leadership Principles in Distance Education

Kathryn S. Atman

Premise

The distance educator who can bridge, successfully, the potential communications gap that hovers between the classroom and the students at remote sites is an individual who understands and applies principles of synergetic leadership both in his/her classroom interactions with students and/or through structured academic advising programs for distance learners.

Motivation, particularly the motivation of students, has been the subject of numerous articles, papers, and books. And yet the subject remains elusive. Knowing techniques of motivation is not enough. Being able to discuss or argue the problem of motivating students under today's societal conditions is not enough. The secret lies somewhere hidden in the chemistry of the personal interaction between the teacher and the learner.

In this paper, we will examine the phenomenon of **synergy**, "combined or cooperative action or force" (Webster's New World Dictionary 1966, p. 1479) or **synergism**, "the simultaneous action of separate agencies which, together, have greater total effect than the sum of their individual effects" (Webster's New World Dictionary 1966, p. 1479). We will also explore the ramifications for distance education of a synergetic campus/off-campus classroom in which the vision of the teacher interacts with the vision of the student in such a manner to release energy in the student, thus enabling the student to change his/her vision into a mission—the dynamic commitment that results in both a course completed and a goal accomplished.

Background of the Synergetic Leadership Model

For the last 25 years, interest in leadership and the application of leadership principles in a variety of settings, e.g., business, industry, education, health-related fields, etc., has escalated. Clearly, the public recognizes the unique nature and attributes of leadership. Peter M. Senge, in *The Fifth Discipline: The Art & Practice of the Learning Organization* (1990), describes the leader/vision relationship in the following manner:

> In a learning organization, leaders may start by pursuing their own vision, but as they learn to listen carefully to others' visions they begin to see that their own personal vision is part of something larger. This does not diminish any leader's sense of responsibility for the vision - if anything it deepens it. "The willingness to abandon your paradigm," says Simon (President and COO, Herman Miller), "comes from your stewardship for the vision."

Being the steward of a vision shifts a leader's relationship toward her or his personal vision. It ceases to be a possession, as in "this is my vision," and becomes a calling. You are "its" as much as it is yours. George Bernard Shaw (1903) expressed the relationship succinctly when he said:

> This is the true joy in life, the being used for a purpose recognized by yourself as a mighty one. . . the being a force of nature instead of a feverish, selfish little clod of ailments and grievances complaining that the world will not devote itself to making you happy. (Senge 1990, 350-352)

Certainly a classroom is a miniature "learning organization," and the concept of the teacher as a 'steward of the vision'—that every student has potential and that every student can achieve—opens the door for a new paradigm that, over time, could alter the face of education. In *The 7 Habits of Highly Effective People,* Stephen R. Covey (1989) has the following to say about the phenomenon of "synergy in the classroom."

> As a teacher, I have come to believe that many truly great classes teeter on the very edge of chaos. Synergy tests whether teachers and students are really open to the principle of the whole being greater than the sum of its parts.

> There are times when neither the teacher nor the student knows for sure what's going to happen. In the beginning, there's a safe environment that enables people to be really open and to learn and to listen to each other's ideas. Then comes brainstorming, where the spirit of evaluation is subordinated to the spirit of creativity, imagining, and intellectual networking. Then an absolutely unusual phenomenon begins to take place. The entire

class is transformed with the excitement of a new thrust, a new idea, a new direction that's hard to define, yet it's almost palpable to the people involved.

Synergy is almost as if a group collectively agrees to subordinate old scripts and to write a new one. (p. 262-265)

A powerful idea! An almost revolutionary idea—when one considers what is happening in most classrooms, both distant and traditional, where the total class format revolves around lecture and content-focused questions and answers.

The Mon Valley Tri-State Leadership Academy

In 1991, the Mon Valley Tri-State Leadership Academy was funded for three years in Morgantown, West Virginia, by the Kellogg Foundation. The Leadership Academy was associated with West Virginia University as well as with the Mon Valley Tri-State Network, an economic development organization serving the region of West Virginia, western Maryland and southwestern Pennsylvania. The purpose of the Academy was to develop leadership and economic development training materials for middle managers and grassroots community leadership in the tri-state area. Faculty for the Academy were drawn from six colleges and universities in the region.

The charge to the leadership curriculum team was to review current leadership literature and to develop a leadership model that synthesized the best of current thinking in the leadership field. Following the literature search, training materials were developed, piloted and evaluated. The Synergetic Leadership Model (Atman and the Mon Valley Tri-State Leadership Academy 1994) was an outgrowth of that work (see Figure 1).

Upon examining the Synergetic Leadership Model, one finds four key features:

1. Leadership begins with the self-examination and self-development of the leader. The leader, as it were, is able to hold him/herself in the palm of the hand with caring, respect, humor and an appreciation for the complexity of the human condition. We all are trying to "muddle through"—one day at a time—and no one is exempt from his/her share of problems.

2. The leader must then make a commitment to the development of the stakeholders (e.g., in a distance education setting, the instructor to the distance learners, and in a basic educational setting, the teacher to the students, the principal to the teachers and the superintendent to the administrators). This involves a willingness to "will another's highest good."

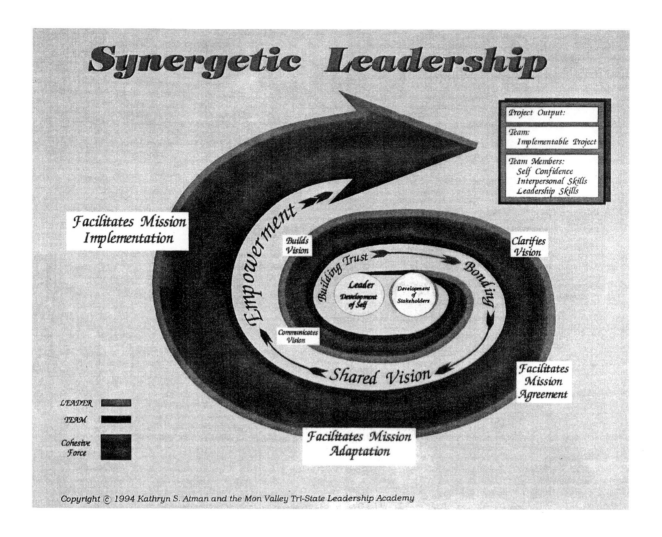

Figure 1.

3. The leader then activates three sets of skills:
   a. Trust building which leads to bonding, shared vision, and empowerment;
   b. Communicating, building, and clarifying the vision;
   c. Translating the vision into the mission which leads to the development of a plan (mission adaptation), and the increasingly successful mission/plan implementation.

4. The vision/mission/plan/goal is accomplished.

Throughout the process, the shared vision, commitment, and combined energy of the leader and the stakeholders—each contributing to the final accomplished goal in his/her unique way—results in the building of a cohesive force. This force can be described as "the simultaneous action of separate agencies which, together, have greater total effect than the sum of their individual effects." The result is **synergy**: joint work, combined or cooperative action or force." In colloquial terms, "the whole becomes greater than the sum of its parts."

In addition to the pilot work at three sites in the tri-state region, the model has been used 1) as a training vehicle to enable adults to develop personal leadership-oriented skills and 2) to teach teachers, supervisors, and tutors how to mentor students. In each case, the pooled energy that comes from commitment and a shared vision has had powerful, positive results.

Psychological and Philosophical Bases of Synergetic Leadership

We now will explore the construct, **Synergetic Leadership,** and consider its implications for distance educators. Several questions will guide this exploration: How can the phenomenon of synergy be made explicit in a distance education classroom? What type of student behaviors are most conducive to academic success in distance education settings? and What teaching characteristics/style/skills will serve distance educators best as they seek to provide high quality courses and programs for students?

A Physics-related Incident. The Synergetic Leadership Model depicts, graphically, the increasing flow of energy from the beginning of a vision, through its translation into a mission and, finally, its resolution as an accomplished goal. A version of the model, rendered in color, shows more clearly the build-up of the cohesive force of energy (a visual sweep of reds and blues) as the project moves from inception to completion. Interlaced with trust, bonding, shared vision, and empowerment, the cohesive action of all elements within the operation of the model results in the project output.

What is this energy and what happens when individuals come together to examine/delve into/explore, together, a new idea? The following paragraphs describe a seminar, conducted by Professor David Bohm, emeritus professor of theoretical physics at Birkbeck College, University of London. Notes from the seminar were transcribed by Donald Factor and later published as a book, *Unfolding Meaning* (Bohm, 1985).

> On the 11th of May, 1984, the group gathered at a small country hotel in the Cotswold village of Mickleton, Gloucestershire, England. Professor Bohm, and his wife Sarah, arrived seeming tired and preoccupied. This was to be his first experience of such a gathering. He had come prepared to give three talks and then to develop his ideas with the group through question and answer sessions. As the weekend unfolded, though, a very different

experience began to emerge for both Professor Bohm and for all the participants.

The sessions developed an atmosphere of contained mutual concern for the revelation of deeper insights. The spirit of friendship and respect between all those present emerged, and this quickly grew into a harmonious field where proposals of many sorts could be collectively investigated in safety and allowed to expand into new levels of understanding.

A dialogue developed in which each participant was able to put aside his own views and listen to those of others. It became increasingly clear that no point of view was in itself complete, and that a collective process of thought was the means by which understanding could be encircled. This fact became the focus of the group's attention. No conclusions were reached nor were any programs initiated; rather the appreciation for the continued unfoldment of new insights of revelation revealed through friendly conversation was seen to be the means by which an increase of harmony might appear. (p. xi, xii)

I would suggest that the phenomenon described in *Unfolding Meaning* is closely akin to the first and second skills inherent in the Synergetic Leadership Model: a) trust building which leads to bonding . . . and b) communicating, building and clarifying the vision. As one reads the book, or listens to a tape recording of the book, he/she is struck by the manner in which the line that usually separates experts from novices (in this case, Bohm from the forty-five participants, whose knowledge level of quantum physics principles varied widely) became blurred. Bohm was always the expert. But his ability to draw others into the dialogue, to make each participant feel valued and to convey respect for the observations and questions of each individual, as evidenced by the recorded dialogue, is striking.

The implications of this vignette? The challenge to distance educators, with students not in the same seminar room but totally separated, is to find the means of 1) bringing all class participants into the dialogue, 2) making each participant feel valued and 3) showing respect for each learner's unique situation and individual differences.

The Mission: "To Go Where We've Never Gone Before." At the point where the vision becomes the mission in a synergetic setting, the cohesive force moves toward empowerment through commitment. How might we consider this phenomenon? One way is through the lens of the conative domain, a little-known psychological domain of behaviors related to striving and volition. The conative domain, identified by German and Scottish faculty psychologists in the late 1700's, was distinguished from the cognitive domain (knowing) and the affective domain (valuing).

Essentially, the conative domain has to do with personal energy and how an individual mobilizes his/her (psychic) energy and sustains the focus of the energy over time. Jung labeled psychic energy ("the intensity with which psychic contents are charged") as libido (Jung 1966) and indicated that psychic contents are either conscious or unconscious and manifest themselves in the life process as conation or desire (Jung 1970).

McDougall's (1932) definition of conation, found in *The Energies of Men,* is more explicit:

> Although our modes of striving are so various, ranging from intense bodily activity to intellectual activity that involves a minimum of bodily expression, we find the same words suitable for describing the striving aspect common to all such activities. We say we are trying, striving, endeavouring, paying keen attention, making an effort, working hard, doing our utmost, exerting ourselves, concentrating all our energies; in technical terms, we are manifesting conation. (p. 117)

The importance of the conative domain in distance education has already been explored (Atman, 1987). In that paper, three areas of distance education were identified as having potential for conative impact: curriculum design, delivery system, and student support services. Of the three areas, student support services has surfaced as the most natural vehicle for a demonstration of the link between the conative domain and the more traditional cognitive, affective, and psychomotor domains. Here, the student takes the step from the vision of his/her personal or professional goal (that can be reached through completion of the distance education course) to the mission: actually registering for the course, picking up the course materials and showing up at the off-campus site for the first session.

The difference between a vision and a mission lies in the intensity level of the commitment. When one has a vision, he/she is able 1) to see beyond the present, 2) to imagine a variety of possibilities, and 3) to identify the one that has the most promise. When one is propelled by a mission, he/she has made a psychic commitment to the vision with a level of intensity that is strong enough to translate the idea into a plan. The conative domain encompasses the wide variety of ways by which we operationalize our plans: e.g., by concentrating all our energies, making an effort, working hard.

What part of ourselves is "in charge" when we concentrate our energies, make the effort, work hard (when another part of ourselves would rather procrastinate or play)? Assagioli (1973) has suggested that this aspect of the personality is the will. Moreover, the will has recognizable attributes: it can be 1) strong (determined and forthright—not weak or willfully obnoxious); 2) skillful ("to apply the existing strength of our will, no matter how small, to act on our imagination, and use its power to realize the great value of having an effective will"); 3) good (as opposed to evil), and 4) transpersonal (capable of altruistic love, humanitarian, and social action) (p. 26-122).

If distance education students are to be successful, they must be able to 1) be "in charge" of themselves, i.e., be able to plan well; 2) use time and resources effectively; and 3) follow through or bring the plan to fruition. This requires the possession of a strong goal orientation. Goal-oriented behavior can be measured. Instruments such as the *Goal Orientation Index (GOI)* (Atman 1986), a self-report inventory that provides a student with a profile of his/her goal accomplishment style, can be useful in pinpointing strengths and weakness in a student's goal-oriented behavior and thereby alerting him/her to possible pitfalls associated with learning at a distance.

It is important that distance educators recognize the unique characteristics of adults as learners. The differences between pedagogy and andragogy (Knowles 1980) are well known. Differences among adults as learners, however, provide a multitude of avenues for exploration. For example, Wlodkowski (1993), in discussing the importance of the adult need for self-determination, has this to say about the complicated issue of intrinsic motivation in adults.

> When adults see themselves as the locus of causality for their learning, they are much more likely to be intrinsically and positively motivated. Adult self-directed personal learning projects have this important ingredient in their natural structure. But once adult learners come face-to-face with instructors in courses, seminars, and training programs, especially if they feel pressured into taking them, the locus of causality may shift away from themselves. Along with that shift goes intrinsic motivation and a sense of self-determination. And here is the rub—for reasons of personal security, this is likely to frequently happen to many adults. They need courses and training, in many instances, not so much because they want them, but because they need the jobs, the promotions, and the money for which these learning experiences are basic requirements. . . Anything we as instructors can do to maximize the perception of adults that the actions they take as learners are their own will meet this need (for self-determination) and has the potential to enhance intrinsic motivation (p. 217-218).

What is the role of the teacher in a context where the intrinsic motivation of the student is an essential ingredient for his/her success? It becomes obvious that the traditional role of the teacher as the authority, dispensing knowledge and providing for skill development, is not sufficient. The enlightened teacher in this context must also be a mentor. Daloz (1986) has identified essential skills in three areas of mentor functioning: 1) support, 2) challenge, and 3) vision. A list of the skills follows:

1. SUPPORT: Listening, providing structure, expressing positive expectations, sharing ourselves, and making it special.

2. CHALLENGE: Setting tasks, engaging in discussion, heating up dichotomies, constructing hypotheses, and setting high standards.

3. VISION: Modeling, keeping tradition, offering a map and suggesting new language (p. 215-235).

A mentor's model, delineating skills related to five well accepted individual growth areas (i.e., intellectual, emotional, social, physical, and psychological), has been proposed (Atman, 1992). Growth in these five areas contribute to the over-all competence and self-determination of individuals and are aspects of the maturation process, identified by Jung as individuation. (Jacobi 1967)

A Walk Along the Edge of the Mystery. The measurement of content knowledge is simple; the measurement of an individual's or group's level of intrinsic motivation is infinitely more complex. But what about the psychic energy dimension of individual or group goal accomplishment? How might we consider that element of synergetic leadership? How do we probe a mystery that can not be seen?

At this point, it may be that the realm of philosophy, not psychology, may provide the best guidance, for here one's world view becomes an important factor in both the questions that one is willing to ask and the answers that one is willing to entertain. The perspective that we will examine in this paper is that of Pierre Teilhard de Chardin, geologist and philosopher. (There are other perspectives that might be pursued, but a comprehensive comparison is beyond the scope of this paper.)

To comprehend the scope of Teilhard's work (which can only be hinted at here), we will ponder two brief selections (written by others) that appear in two of Teilhard's books: *The Divine Milieu* (1957) and *Human Energy* (1962). The first selection, written by N. M. Wilders, is quoted from the Foreword found in *Human Energy*.

> It will become increasingly evident that Teilhard's work as a whole has a profound unity and develops a primary intuition. On the occasion of a lecture on the subject on 'The Philosophical Intuition' given at Bologna on 10 April, 1911, Henri Bergson strikingly demonstrated that there are two ways of approaching a philosopher's work: 'A philosophical system seems at first to stand up like a complete building of skilled architecture, in which arrangements have been made for the comfortable accommodation of all problems. It is possible to consider this edifice from the outside, to go all round it, to examine each of its features separately and identify the materials used by its maker and the source from which he obtained them. This method may be

useful, though it tells us very little about its internal coherence and the motives that determined its overall conception.

There is however a second way of approach to a thinker's work. This is to penetrate to the very heart of the building, "to take our place in the philosopher's mind." Then the system undergoes a total transformation. The coherence and necessity of all its elements become suddenly perceptible. "Then everything converges to a single point, to which we feel we can draw closer and closer, though we must despair of ever reaching it" (Danielou, 1962). All this very largely applies to the work of Teilhard de Chardin. In his case also, it is not enough to consider his work from outside and examine the elements of which it is built one by one, though this effort to study his work in some way from within, and discover the central point from which the author has built and which has given him perpetual new inspirations.

Putting aside his theological writing, it is apparent that the point of departure of Teilhard's whole work is the wish to penetrate as deeply as possible into the fundamental structure of the universe in which we live and of which we form part. More than any other philosopher, he took the findings of the sciences as his starting point, since these enabled him to grasp the work in its historical dimension. From this point of view—which to him became evidential—he tried to discover the inner coherence and essential direction of universal history, which, despite the multitude and diversity of phenomena, reveals to his eyes a fundamental unity and harmony which guide even our activity as men in that direction.

All his essays start from this primal conviction and try to show us the nature of that fundamental unity and the prospects it opens up on human existence. Bergson's words apply also to him: 'The whole complexity of his teaching, which might stretch to infinity, is therefore only the incommensurability between his simple intuition and the means of expressing it that are at his disposal.' I do not think we should be far from Teilhard's primal intuition if we were to seek it in the neighborhood of what he called the law of progressive complexity and increasing consciousness, in other words the problem of the relation between spirit and matter. (pp. 9-11)

A philosophical position, no matter how sound, should not be examined apart from the mind and heart of the philosopher. In short, "the words and the music must match." To consider the extent to which the words of the philosophical system match the person of the philosopher, we now turn to "Teilhard de Chardin: The Man," a selection written by Pierre Leroy, S.J., that appears as a statement prior to the preface of *The Divine Milieu* (1957).

The look in his eyes when they met your eyes revealed the man's soul: his reassuring sympathy restored your confidence in yourself. Just to speak to him made you feel better; you knew that he was listening to you and that he understood you. His own faith was in the invincible power of love: men hurt one another by not loving one another. And this was not naiveté but the goodness of the man, for he was good beyond the common measure. In him, this belief was no mere conventional sentiment grafted on a generous nature, but the fruit of long meditation; it was a certainty that came only with years of reflection. It was this deep-seated spiritual conviction that led Pere Pierre Teilhard de Chardin to the practice of self-forgetfulness: self being forgotten in a sympathetic union with all men and with every individual man. (p. 13)

Teilhard de Chardin (1957) envisioned individuals, their world, and the universe as a whole—not as fragmented parts. And although many officials in his own church did not support his philosophical position, he remained steadfast in his faith. Even today, not all people may agree with his world-view, but his belief gave him a perspective that enabled him to relate in a unique manner to other individuals. He wrote:

> . . . God reveals himself everywhere, beneath our groping efforts, as a *universal milieu,* only because he is the *ultimate point* on which all realities converge. . . However vast the divine *milieu* may be, it is in reality a *centre.* It therefore has the properties of a centre, and above all the absolute and final power to unite (and consequently to complete) all beings within its breast. In the divine *milieu* all the elements of the universe *touch each other* by that which is most inward and ultimate in them. There they shed, in their meeting, the mutual externality and the incoherence which form the basic pain of human relationships. (p. 114)

The energy dimension of Teilhard de Chardin's philosophical position was further developed in *Human Energy* (1962) in a section titled "The Nature and Dimensions of Human Energy."

> By the energy of man I here mean the always increasing portion of cosmic energy at present undergoing the recognizable influence of the centers of human activity.
>
> a. <u>Incorporated energy</u> is that which the slow biological evolution of the earth has gradually accumulated and harmonized in our organism of flesh and nerves: the astonishing 'natural machine' of the human body.

b. <u>Controlled energy</u> is the energy around him which man ingeniously succeeds in dominating with physical power originating from his limbs by means of 'artificial machines.'

c. <u>Spiritualized energy</u>, lastly, is localized in the immanent zones of our free activity, and forms the stuff of our intellectual processes, affections and volitions. This energy is probably incapable of measurement, but is very real all the same, since it gains a reflective and passionate mastery of things and their relationships. (p. 115)

How much easier it is to send a message by FAX instead of by ship or pony express. We are the beneficiaries of the products of our imaginative minds—particularly in the area of technology, "the pack horse" of distance education.

By now I anticipate that there are those readers who are questioning the need to raise philosophical questions. Why should we, indeed? Who wants to assume any risk by raising questions that might be controversial? But I would argue that educators must do it if only because of the nature of the problems facing our educational institutions. The lead article in the April, 1995, issue of the *Phi Delta KAPPAN* describes existing conditions in schools graphically: "Let's Declare Education A Disaster and Get On With Our Lives" (Smith, 1995). In this frank article, Smith begins by stating:

I have a serious suggestion to make. We should stop worrying about the problems of education, declare it a disaster, and let teachers and students get on with their lives. The trouble with the endless concern over "problems" in education is that many well-meaning but often misguided and sometimes meddlesome people believe that solutions must exist. They waste their own and other people's time and energy trying to find and implement these solutions. Typically, they try harder to do more of something that is already being done (although what is being done is probably one of the problems).

However, if education is a disaster, then it is not a collection of problems to be "solved," and trying to "improve what we are already doing will only make the situation worse. You don't find solutions to disasters—you try to extricate yourself and other people from them. The way to survive a disaster is to do something different. (p. 584)

Somehow, on the road to the 21st Century, basic education has lost its way. Can distance education avoid this pitfall?

Charting the Course for Communication in Distance Education

I have raised the philosophical question, because at the core of Synergetic Leadership is a commitment to the development of stakeholders and a willingness to work with each of them to assure his/her success. In a materialistic society, who in his/her right mind would choose to empower someone else? Only the individual who 1) understands something about the fragility as well as the complexity of the human condition, 2) holds every human being within a perspective that values harmony—and integrity—and 3) believes that every individual has a gift that he/she can use to contribute to the well being and betterment of society, regardless of the status of that individual at the present time.

Distance educators are acutely aware of the need to be responsive to the needs of their students. Jung's theory of psychological type is one approach to understanding individual differences in people (Atman, 1990). Research of Davis (1995) substantiates the value of this approach to student needs—particularly student needs that can be linked to the use of the technology itself.

As we consider charting a new course for distance (and general) education, we return to Senge (1990) for additional insight on the role of the leader as a teacher.

> . . . leaders in learning organizations . . . focus predominantly on purpose and systemic structure. Moreover, they "teach" people throughout the organization to do likewise.
>
> Systemic structure is the domain of systems thinking and mental models. At this level, leaders are continually helping people see the big picture: how different parts of the organization interact, how different situations parallel one another because of common underlying structures, how local actions have longer-term and broader impacts than local actors often realize, and why certain operating policies are needed for the system as a whole. But despite its importance, the level of systemic structure is not enough. By itself, it lacks a sense of purpose. It deals with the *how* and not the *why*.
>
> By focusing on the "purpose story"—the larger explanation of why the organization exists and where it is trying to head - leaders add an additional dimension of meaning. They provide what philosophy calls a "teleological explanation" (from the Greek *telos.* meaning "end" or "purpose")—an understanding of what we are trying to become. When people throughout an organization come to share in a larger sense of purpose, they are united in a common destiny. They have a sense of continuity and identity not achievable in any other way. (p. 353-354)

The power is in the vision, the "story," the sense of purpose, and the opportunity to become a part of something larger than ourselves. Somehow, we must recapture that dimension of the educational process for ourselves and for our students.

Synergetic Leadership and Distance Education

A powerful, new paradigm is needed if we are to step beyond classroom/site communication problems. I propose that Synergetic Leadership, as a personification of the Conative Domain, exemplifies such a paradigm shift. Through this newly constituted lens we can envision a future classroom where the students as well as the teacher are all learners: captivated by the exploration of new ideas yet buttressed by a solid knowledge foundation in the concepts, principles, and methodologies found in the relevant disciplines. Fortunately, this "future classroom" is already present in some distance education programs—through instructors who personalize in spite of distance/technology.

The key to the success of this "new" classroom is the distance educator: knowledgeable in his/her academic field, flexible and caring in the approach taken to involve students actively in the learning process, and filled with curiosity and enthusiasm as he/she advances into the 21st century with grace and confidence.

References

Assagioli, R. 1973. *The Act of Will*. New York: Penguin.

Atman, K. S. 1986. *Goal Orientation Index*. Pittsburgh, PA: University of Pittsburgh.

Atman, K. S. 1987. The role of conation (striving) in the distance education enterprise. *The American Journal of Distance Education* 1(1):14–24.

Atman, K. S. 1990. Psychological type elements and goal accomplishment style: Implications for distance education. In *Contemporary Issues in American Distance Education,* ed. M. G. Moore, 136–150. Oxford: Pergamon Press.

Atman, K. S. 1992. Curriculum implications of goal accomplishment style for design technology education. Paper presented at the International Conference on Design and Technology Educational Research and Curriculum Development, Loughborogh, England.

Bohm, D. 1985. *Unfolding Meaning*. London: Routledge Kegan Paul, Inc.

Covey, S. R. 1989. *The 7 Habits of Highly Effective People: Powerful Lessons in Personal Change*. New York: Fireside.

Daloz, L. A. 1986. *Effective Teaching and Mentoring*. San Francisco: Jossey-Bass, Inc.

Davis, M. 1995. The interrelationship of conation, goal accomplishment style and psychological type in distance learners. Ed.D. diss. West Virginia University, Morgantown, W. Virginia.

Jacobi, Jolande. 1967. *The Way of Individuation*. New York: Harcourt, Brace & World, Inc.

Jung, C. G. 1966. *Two Essays on Analytical Psychology*. Princeton, NJ: Princeton University Press.

Jung, C. G. 1970. The theory of psychoanalysis. *Collected Works of C. G. Jung*. 4:111–28.

Knowles, M. S. 1980. *The Modern Practice of Adult Education: From Pedagogy to Andragogy*. Chicago: Follett.

McDougall, W. 1932. *The Energies of Men*. New York: Charles Scribner's Sons.

Senge, P. M. 1990. *The Fifth Discipline: The Art & Practice of The Learning Organization*. New York: Bantam Doubleday Dell Publishing Group, Inc.

Smith, F. 1995. Let's declare education a disaster and get on with our lives. *Phi Delta KAPPAN* 76(8):584.

Teilhard de Chardin, P. 1957. T*he Divine Milieu*. New York: Harper & Row.

Teilhard de Chardin, P. 1962 (English translation, 1969). *Human Energy*. London: William Collins Sons & Co. Ltd.

Webster's New World Dictionary (College Edition). 1966. Toronto, Ontario: Nelson, Foster and Scott, Ltd.

Wlodkowski, R. J. 1993. *Enhancing Adult Motivation to Learn*. San Francisco: Jossey-Bass, Inc.

Notes on Authors

Kathryn S. Atman is an Associate Professor at the University of Pittsburgh. Address: University of Pittsburgh, 4730 Forbes Quadrangle, Pittsburgh, PA 15260.

Roger Bruning is Co-Director of the Center for Instructional Innovation at the University of Nebraska-Lincoln. Address: University of Nebraska-Lincoln, 1301 Seaton Hall, Lincoln, NE 68588-0641.

Michaeleen A. Davis is an Assistant Professor of Elementary Education at Indiana State University. Address: Indiana State University, 818 School of Education, Terre Haute, IN 47809.

Catherine Fulford is Assistant Professor of Educational Technology at the University of Hawaii. Address: University of Hawaii, 1776 University Avenue, Wist 230, Honolulu, HI 96822.

Yoland Gayol is a Project Assistant at The American Center for the Study of Distance Education at The Pennsylvania State University. Address: The Pennsylvania State University, The American Center for the Study of Distance Education, 403 S. Allen Street, Suite 206, University Park, PA 16801-5202.

Chère Campbell Gibson is an Associate Professor in the Department of Continuing and Vocational Education at the University of Wisconsin-Madison. Address: University of Wisconsin-Madison, 1300 Linden Drive, Madison, WI 53706.

Susan May is Assistant Professor and Chair of the Adult Education Department at St. Francis Xavier University. Address: St. Francis Xavier University, Box 5000, Antigonish, Nova Scotia, Canada B2G 2T4.

Christine H. Olgren is Distance Education Outreach Manager at the University of Wisconsin-Madison. Address: University of Wisconsin-Madison, 225 N. Mills St., Room 112, Madison, Wisconsin 53706.

Rudy Pugliese is an Assistant Professor in the Department of Professional and Technical Communication in the the College of Liberal Arts at the Rochester Institute of Technology. Address: Rochester Institute of Technology, 1 Lomb Memorial Drive, Rochester, New York 14623.

Shuqiang Zhang is an Assistant Professor in the Department of Educational Psychology at the University of Hawaii. Address: University of Hawaii-Manoa, Department of Educational Psychology, 1776 University Ave., Wist 208, Honolulu, HI 96822.

This monograph was developed and produced by Margaret A. Koble with the assistance of Kathy J. Barrickman. Address: The Pennsylvania State University, The American Center for the Study of Distance Education, 110 Rackley Building, University Park, PA 16802.

The American Journal of Distance Education

The American Journal of Distance Education is published by the American Center for the Study of Distance Education at The Pennsylvania State University. **The Journal** is designed for professional trainers; teachers in schools, colleges and universities; researchers; adult educators; and other specialists in education and communications. Created to disseminate information and act as a forum for criticism and debate about research in and the practice of distance education in the Americas, **The Journal** provides reports of new research, discussions of theory, and program developments in the field. **The Journal** is issued three times a year.

SELECTED CONTENTS

For information write to:
The American Journal of Distance Education
The Pennsylvania State University
110 Rackley Building
University Park, PA 16802
Tel: (814) 863-3764   Fax: (814) 865-5878